LITTLE BOOK OF

ISSEY MIYAKE

Published in 2025 by Welbeck
An Imprint of HEADLINE PUBLISHING GROUP LIMITED

Cataloguing in Publication Data is available from the British Library

ISBN 9781035420636

Printed in China

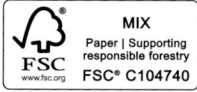

HEADLINE PUBLISHING GROUP LIMITED
An Hachette UK Company
Carmelite House
50 Victoria Embankment
London EC4Y 0DZ

The authorised representative in the EEA is Hachette Ireland,
8 Castlecourt Centre, Dublin 15, D15 XTP3, Ireland (email: info@hbgi.ie)

www.headline.co.uk
www.hachette.co.uk

LITTLE BOOK OF

ISSEY MIYAKE

The story of the iconic fashion designer

KATI CHITRAKORN

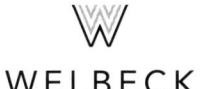

WELBECK

CONTENTS

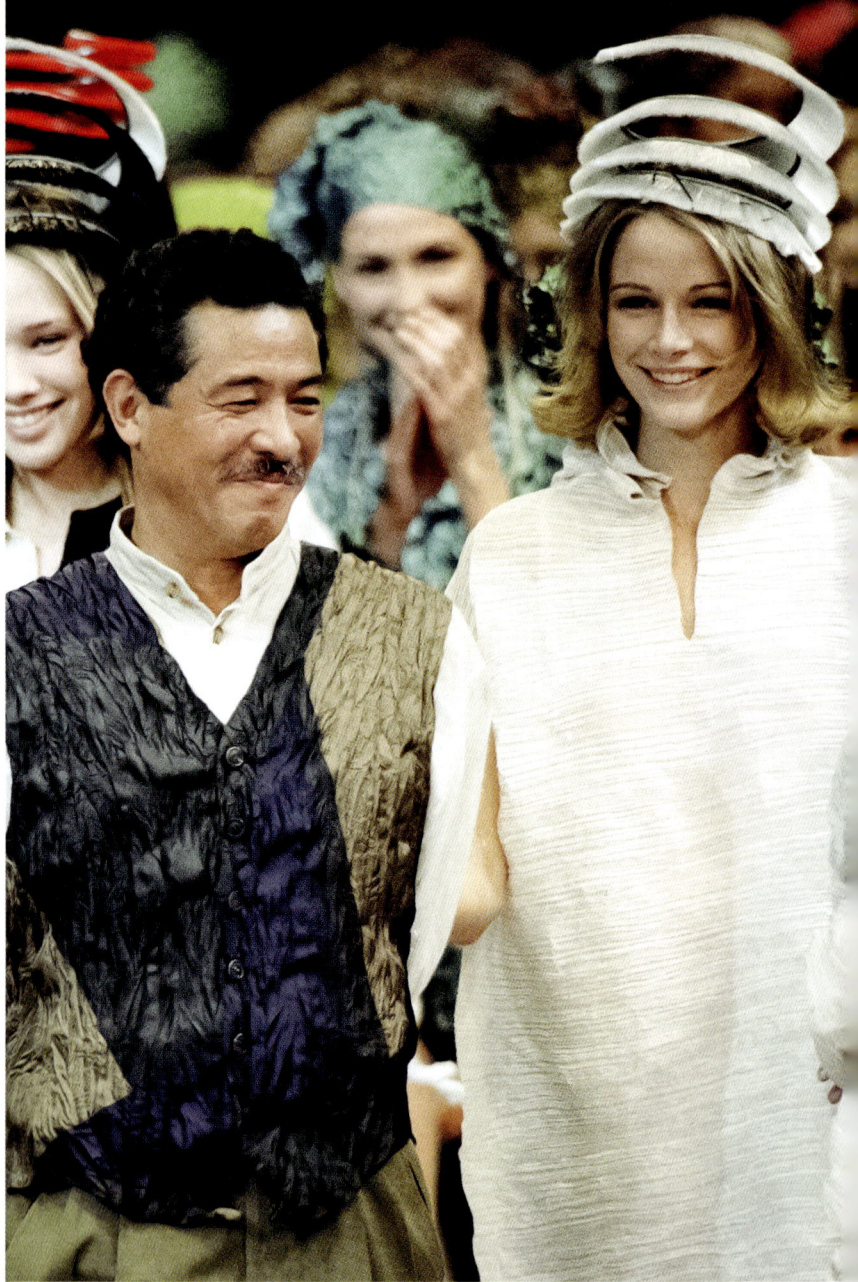

INTRODUCTION

"Clothes are of no interest except insofar as they provoke sentiments and reactions in those who wear them. I create, not to express my ego, my personality, but to try and bring answers to those who are asking themselves questions about our age and how we should live in it."

Those were the words offered by Issey Miyake for the catalogue of the "Making Things" exhibition at the Fondation Cartier pour l'Art Contemporain in Paris in 1998, and a maxim that the designer abided by, with the liberating and innovative garments that defined his career.

Known as the "designer's designer", Miyake has always maintained that he was interested not in fashion but in design for living. He cared about the relationship between people and the clothing that covered their bodies. Informed and influenced by a multitude of disciplines, including a cross-pollination of cultures and industries, Miyake bridged tradition with modernity and redefined what clothing – and beauty – could be.

One of the first Japanese fashion designers to show his collections internationally, he shunned conventional Western ideas of beauty and sexiness, which were preoccupied with accentuating and revealing the human form. Instead, he was more interested in the idea of freedom in clothing, the space

OPPOSITE Issey Miyake and models at his show for A/W 1994, in Paris.

it occupies and its relationship with the body. Indeed, his designs focus on mobility and comfort.

His work evolved across five distinct periods, with each chapter characterized by a relentless pursuit of innovation. From his commitment to experimenting with technology and materials, Miyake remained curious, pioneering the use of pleats that later became part of his celebrated Pleats Please line and unique styles like the Bao Bao bags. His approach won over fans like Apple's co-founder Steve Jobs, whose trademark black turtleneck sweaters were designed by Miyake.

At a time when fashion and art were often regarded as wholly separate practices, Miyake promoted a liaison between the two, giving new meaning to collaborations. He counted architect Isamu Noguchi and photographer Irving Penn among his biggest influences. Miyake also fostered new talent and passed forward what he had learned from his colleagues and collaborators after many years of experimentation.

Miyake "retired" from the fashion industry before the millennium to devote himself to research and special projects. While he handed over the design process to trusted associates, the company remained privately owned and he continued to oversee all the collections. His many awards included Japan's Order of Culture (2010), while in France he was appointed a Chevalier of the Légion d'honneur in 1993 (advanced to Commandeur in 2016).

On August 5, 2022, Miyake died of liver cancer aged 84, but his influence lives on, across his own empire which today includes ready-to-wear, bags, fragrance and various sub-lines and through the generations of designers that followed him and his views of fashion as a space for limitless experimentation and imagination.

OPPOSITE From S/S 1990, shown in Paris.

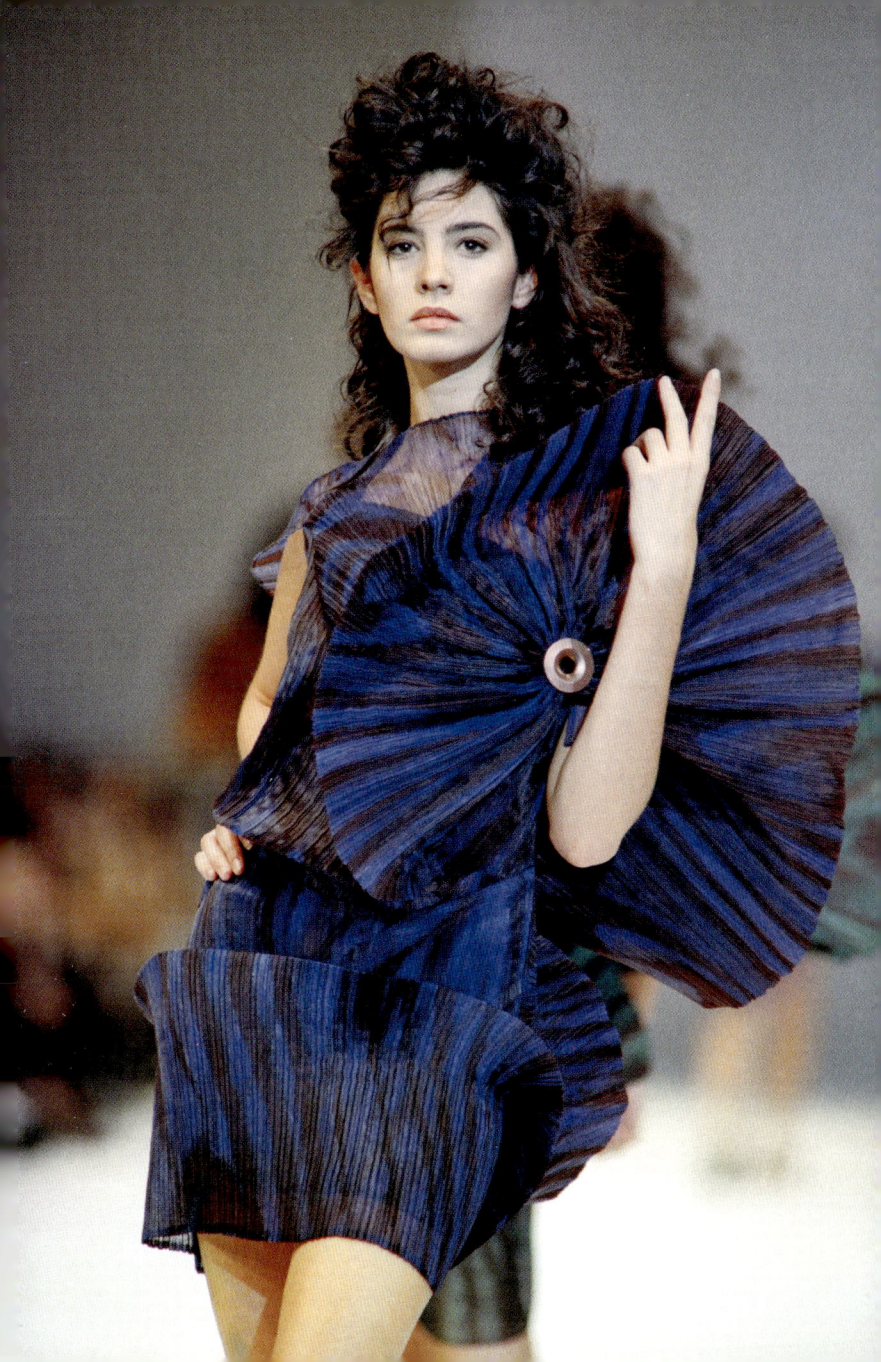

EARLY YEARS

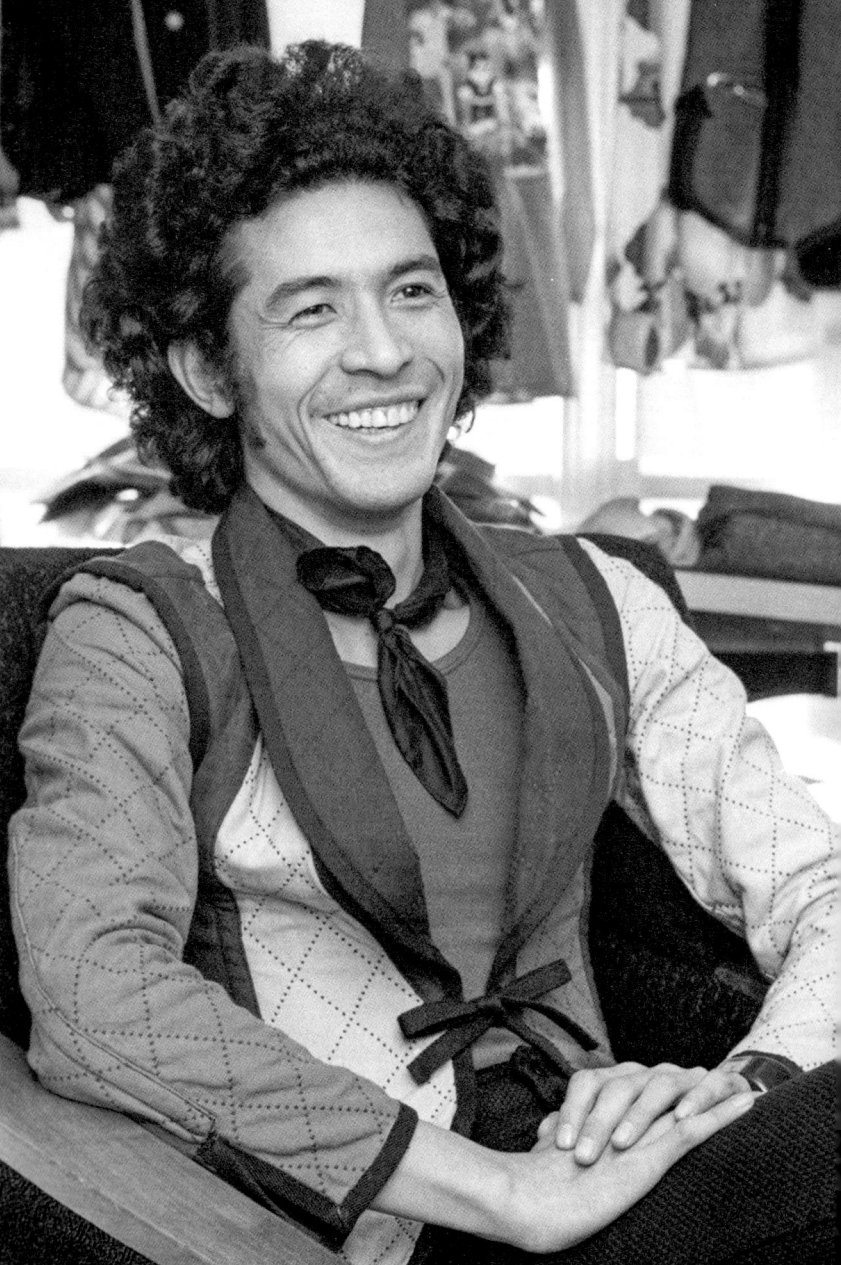

A CREATIVE VISION

Born Kazunaru Miyake in 1938, Issey Miyake became interested in design after coming across the two bridges created by the artist and architect Isamu Noguchi in his hometown, Hiroshima. At the time, Miyake attended Hiroshima Kokutaiji High School in the city's Naka Ward and this marked the first moment he felt a desire to create. Seeing the bridges in the epicentre of the attack towards the end of the Second World War led Miyake to observe that design could evoke emotion and instil feelings of hope and freedom amid destruction. Years later, he would form a deep connection with Noguchi and collaborative exhibitions presented the work of the two men.

M iyake was just seven years old when he survived the Hiroshima bombing. His father, a Japanese army officer, died on duty. His mother died of radiation poisoning three years later, although he rarely spoke about it. "I tried never to be defined by my past. I did not want to be labelled 'the designer who survived the atomic bomb', and therefore I have always avoided questions about Hiroshima. They made me uncomfortable," he wrote for the *New York Times* in 2009.

OPPOSITE Issey Miyake in October 1971.

At the age of 10, Miyake developed a bone marrow disease as the result of radiation exposure which left him with a permanent limp. Between 1945 and 1952, when Japan was occupied by the Americans, it was poor Japanese men who first became fascinated by the Ivy League fashion that was worn by soldiers off duty. The popularity of Ivy style, which included classic pieces such as Oxford or button-down shirts, sweater vests, khaki trousers and penny loafers, later took off more widely, permeating Japanese youth culture in the 1960s.

As a teenager, Miyake took an interest in making things. He first aspired to be a painter, but then became fascinated by fashion, despite this not being considered an appropriate subject for men in Japan to study in the 50s. In 1959, he enrolled at Tama Art University in Tokyo and majored in graphic design because fashion was not offered as a course of study.

When the World Design Conference was held in Tokyo for the first time in May 1960, he famously wrote a letter of protest to the president of the Japanese executive committee Junzo Sakakura, describing the conference as "unacceptable" because clothing design was not included in the programme. Miyake believed there needed to be a clear distinction between "trend" and "fashion", or clothing, which he felt merited as much attention as other design subjects.

After graduating in the summer of 1965, Miyake went to Paris, where he trained at the École de la Chambre Syndicale de la Couture Parisienne. An original sketch by the designer from this time shows a boxy short-sleeved red dress with a yellow turned-up collar that mimicked the popular straight-cut shift dresses of the era. The decision to leave his home country and move to the other side of the world was unusual at the time, but Miyake had an open mind and wanted to explore different ways of life.

OPPOSITE Issey Miyake and a model wearing his S/S 1973 collection.

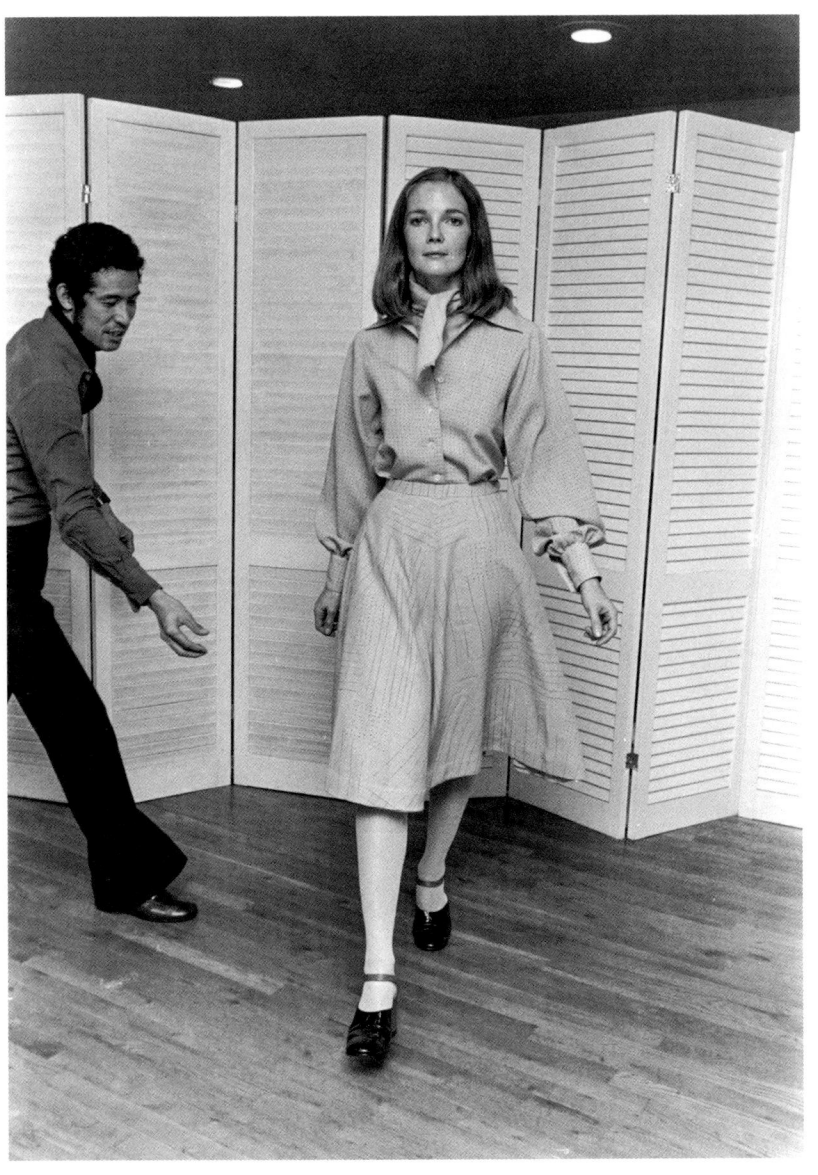

Miyake's first jobs were in the studios of Guy Laroche and Hubert de Givenchy. There, he mastered classic tailoring and the kind of draping used in haute couture to create beautiful clothes for the wealthy. But his mindset shifted after experiencing the Paris riots of 1968, which led to the closure of haute couture houses including that of Cristóbal Balenciaga. (The company relaunched in 2021 after being acquired by the Bogart Group and is today owned by Kering.)

The social unrest consequently sparked a fresh air of unconformity and new creativity among French fashion designers such as Sonia Rykiel. For Miyake, the events served as a kind of awakening: he lost interest in designing for the upper classes and wanted to create clothing for "the many rather than for the few", he told the *Wall Street Journal* in 2012. "I wanted to make clothing that was as universal as jeans and T-shirts."

He moved to New York for a brief stint, where he worked for fashion designer Geoffrey Beene as an assistant designer, channelling the rebellious youth spirit he had witnessed into designs that also embraced the mood of the era, such as shift dresses and short hemlines – as seen via his sketches for the house. He also met with artists Robert Rauschenberg, Claes Oldenburg and Jasper Johns, before returning in 1970 to Tokyo.

Back home, Miyake received commissions from big companies including the Japanese cosmetics firm Shiseido, who asked him to create designs for corporate clothing for the Osaka Expo, and the Japanese textile corporation Toray Industries, for which he took part in the Toray Knit Exhibition. There, his interests in technology and materials began to form, as he designed modular garments with components that could be assembled and disassembled. The designer called it "constructible fashion".

Miyake founded the Miyake Design Studio in April 1970 with the help of Tomoko Komuru, who became his longstanding business partner, and Makiko Minagawa, a textile designer. Miyake had turned 31 and after years of invaluable experience he was ready to start working. After his experience of America, Miyake became fixated with the idea of freedom, which became a key concept in the studio, where he worked with his team to explore the relationship between clothing and the body.

From the outset, an essential tenet of Miyake's work has been making clothing from "a piece of cloth", a creative process that uses only one piece of fabric to create a new design. Miyake was inspired by the kimono which, in contrast to the construction of Western clothing, is composed of rectangular pieces of flat material that are draped over the body.

"All of my work stems from the simplest of ideas that go back to the earliest civilizations: making clothing from one piece of cloth. It is my touchstone. I believe that all forms of creativity are related," Miyake told the *New York Times* in 2014. "Clothing," Miyake sought to remind the world then, is the word that he prefers to "fashion". "I am most interested in people and the human form," he said. "Clothing is the closest thing to all humans."

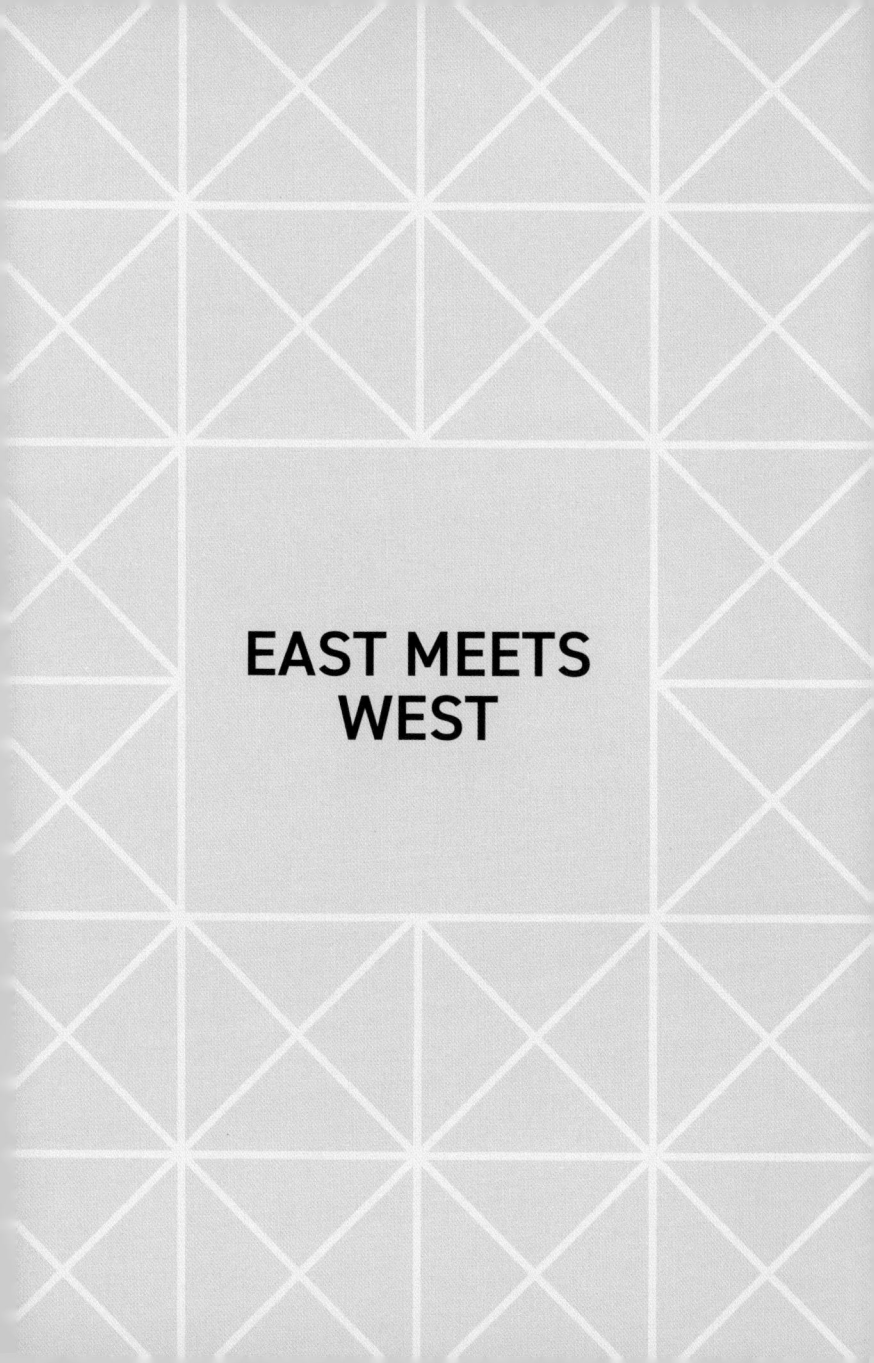

EAST MEETS WEST

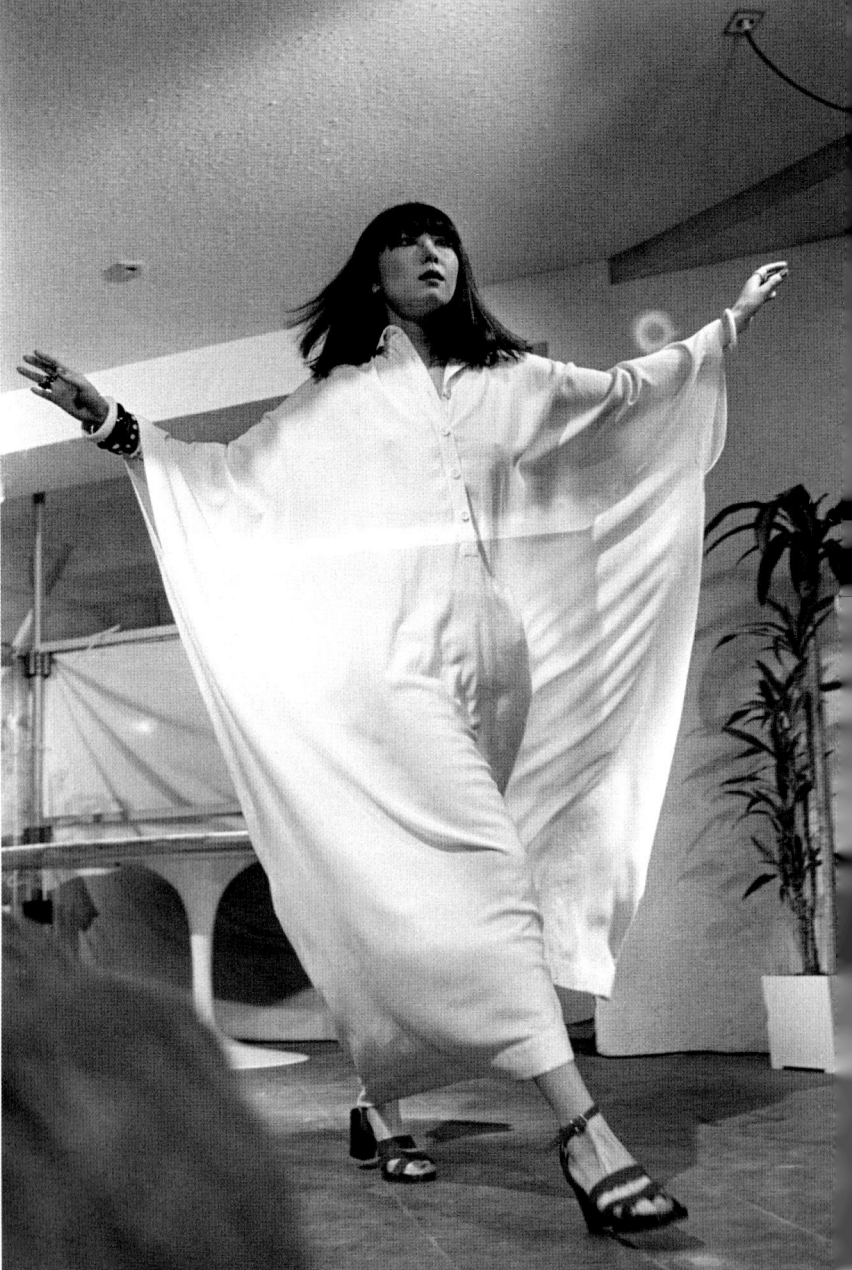

A NEW APPROACH

Miyake's early collections took inspiration from rural Japan: he used the check pattern from farmers' clothes, often made from a cotton crepe fabric that had been dipped in the cold waters of Northern Japan, and other traditional fabrics and techniques that were no longer commonly used, such as *shijira-ori*, a cooling sweat-absorbing fabric, and *sashiko*, a form of embroidery used for repair and reinforcement, which had been used in Japan since the Nara period in the eighth century. Traditional farmers' outfits were rooted in practicality and durability, qualities that seemed contrary to the conventional refinement of the high-end fashion world.

One of the first known Miyake photoshoots took place at Ueno Station in Tokyo, featuring models among female farmers who were bringing vegetables into the city. As a provincial boy from Hiroshima, Miyake identified with – and respected – these hard-working women.

Within a year of launching his studio, Miyake presented the first small collection under his name in New York. For Spring/Summer 1971, he created the handkerchief dress, a one-size dress made using three square pieces of jersey cloth, with the bias used to cross the shoulder straps in the back. It marked a continuation of his "one piece of cloth" premise, where clothes are crafted from a single roll of textile.

OPPOSITE From S/S 1974.

RIGHT Models
backstage at the
show for A/W 1989.

OPPOSITE Actress
and model Monica
Bellucci wears
a body stocking
designed by Issey
Miyake.

OVERLEAF Models
on the runway for
S/S 1975.

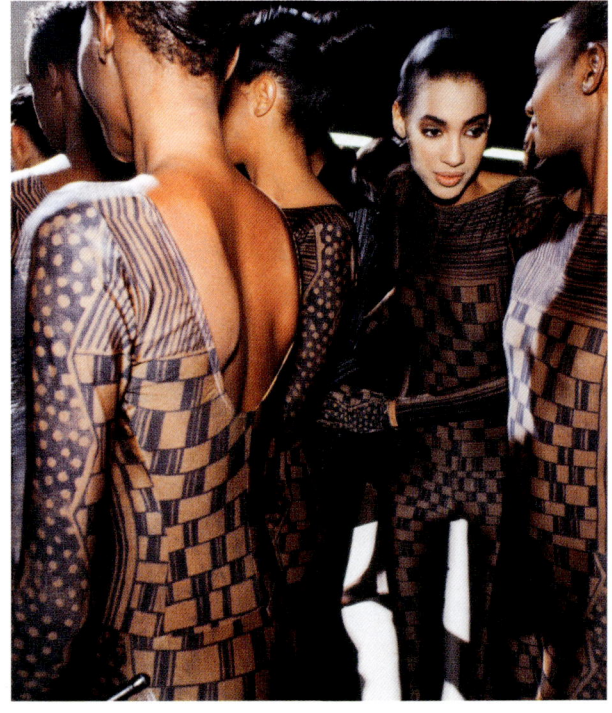

For Autumn/Winter 1971, Miyake worked with the artist
Makiko Minagawa to create a jersey cloth dress printed with a
Japanese-style tattoo of Janis Joplin and Jimi Hendrix. It was
inspired by traditional Japanese tattoos made in homage to the
dead. Minagawa later joined Miyake in his studio and worked
with the designer for over three decades. The dress is now
part of the collection at the highly regarded Kyoto Costume
Institute in Japan.

Miyake's early collections caught the eye of Diana Vreeland,
the iconic editor-in-chief of *Vogue*, who gave him a page in the
magazine. US department store Bloomingdale's also agreed to
sell some of his designs.

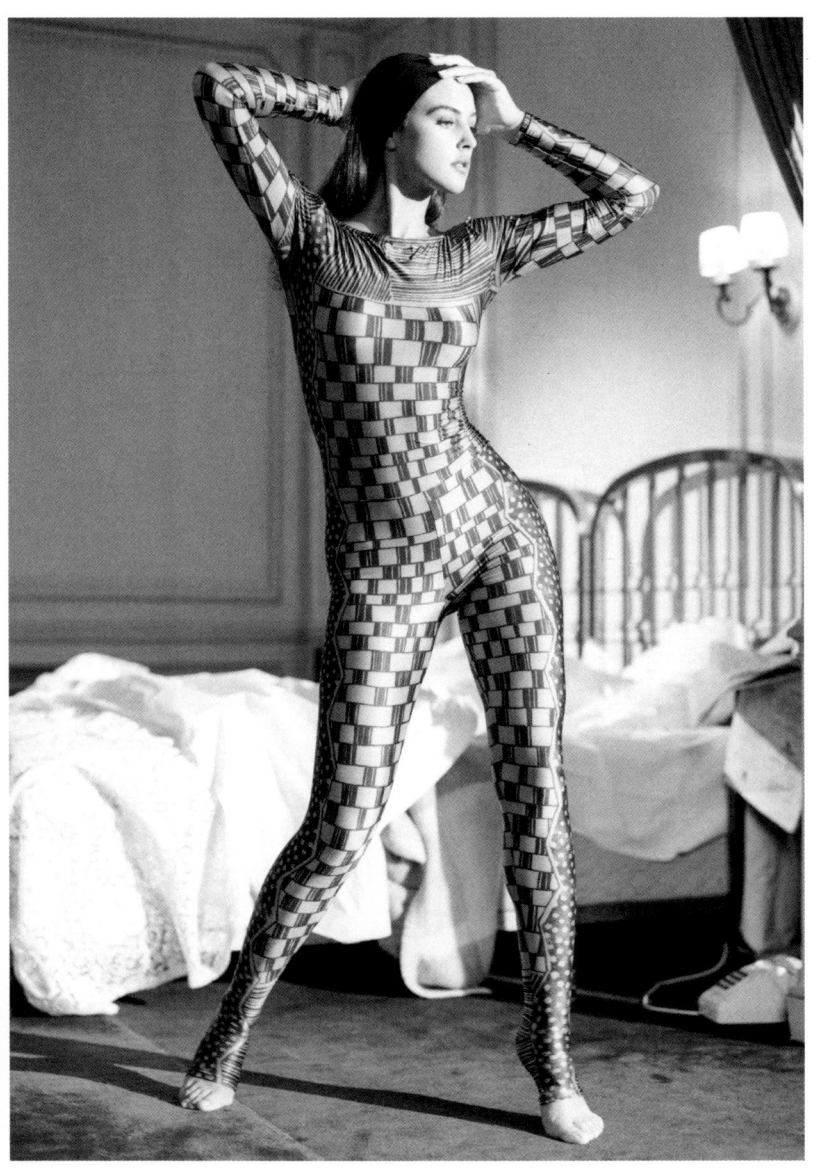

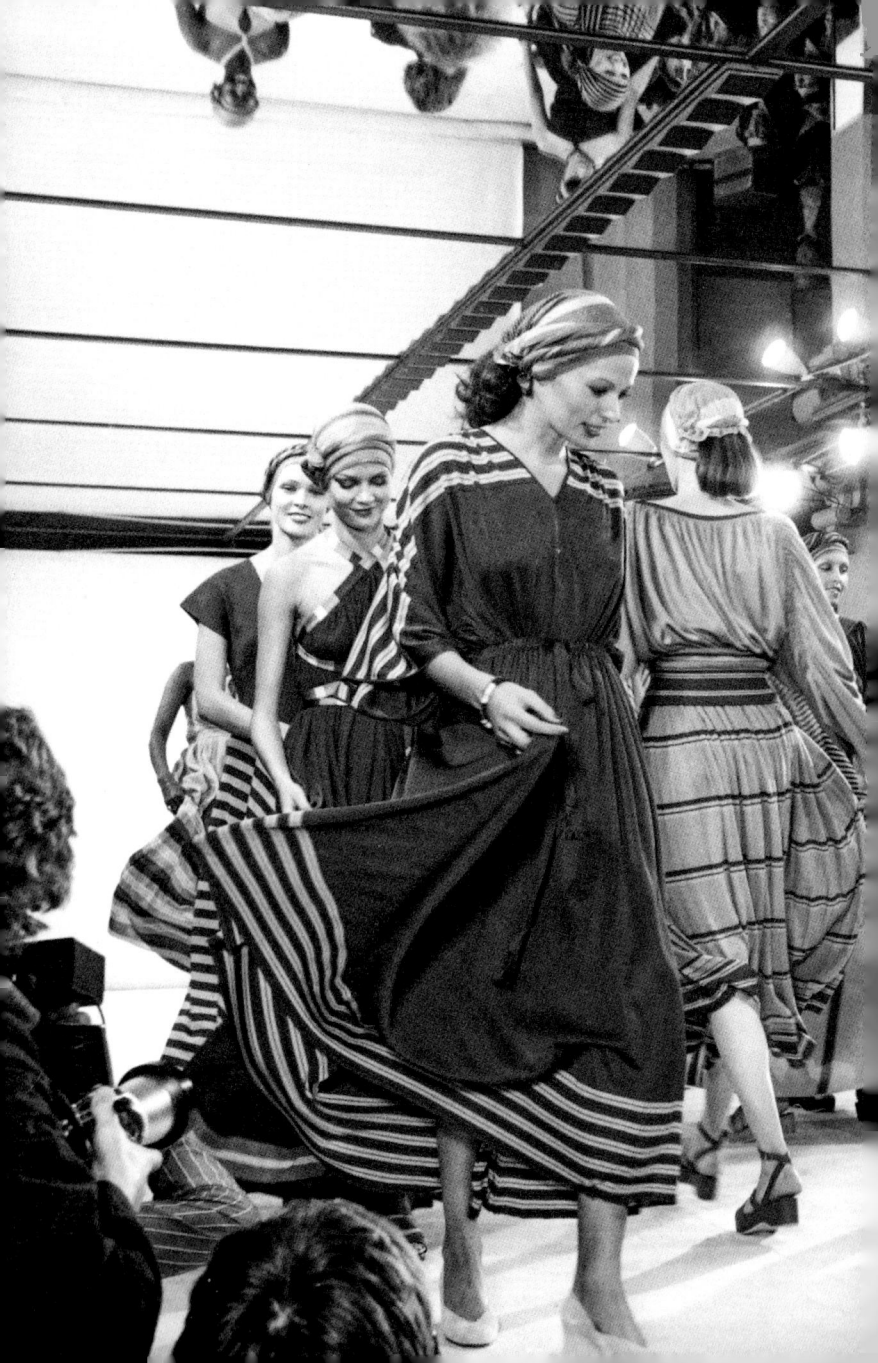

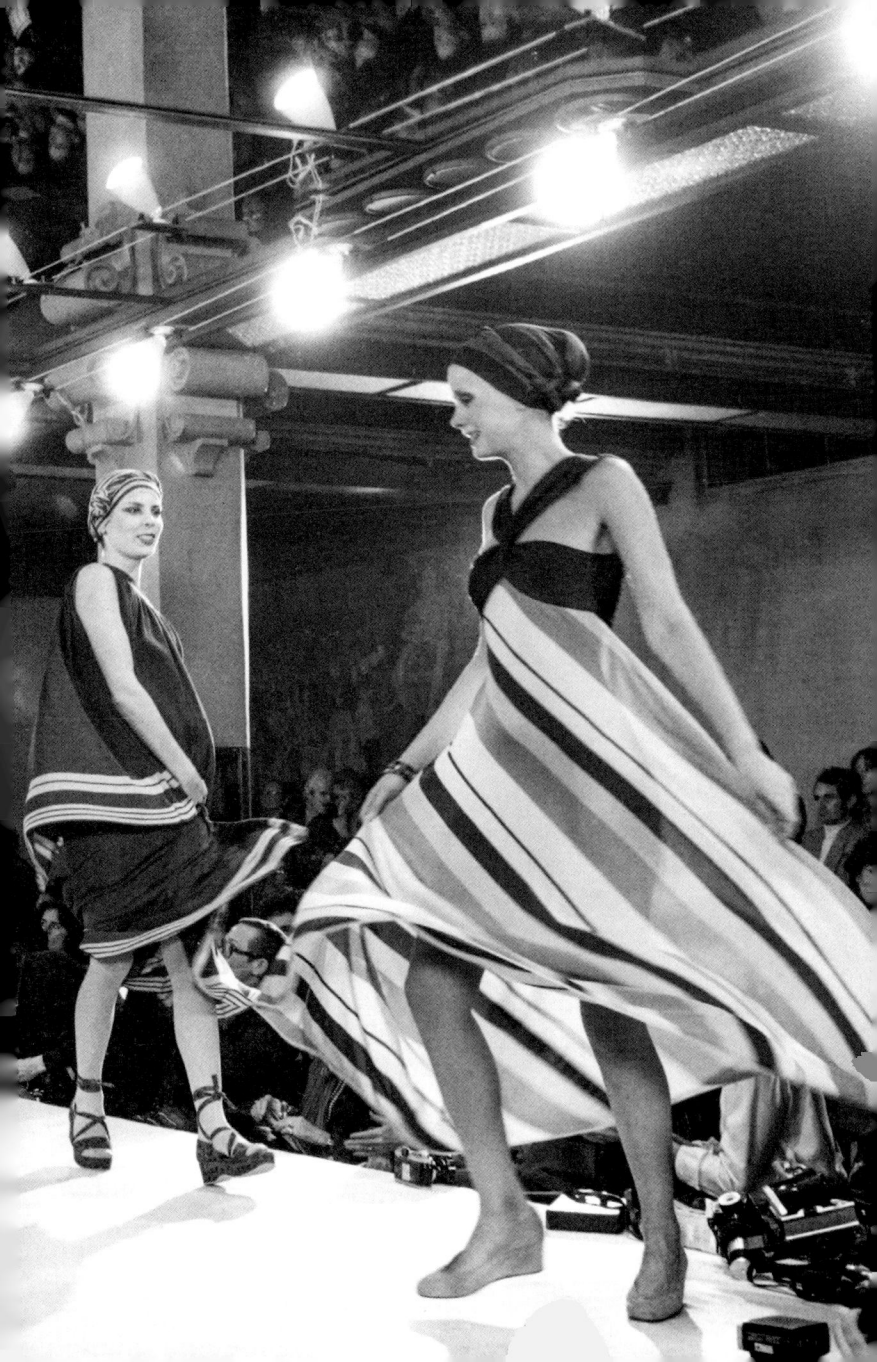

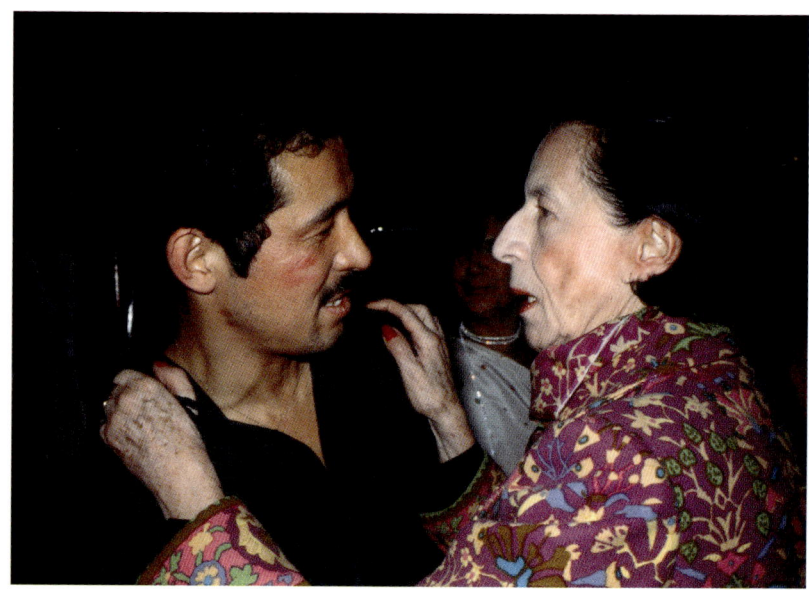

ABOVE Issey Miyake
and fashion editor
Diana Vreeland
in conversation
at Studio 54,
New York, in 1978.

"Issey is a fabric expert," Vreeland wrote for the introduction of *Issey Miyake: East Meets West*, a book published in 1978 that summarized Miyake's work up to 1977. "He believes that only by knowing well the basic tradition of a craft can one breakaway and run either on-base or off, expressing successfully new ideas and at the same time being totally one's self. He has the courage of the Japanese and is proud to be Japanese."

Vreeland was one of many influential editors that Miyake would win over in his lifetime. She continued: "I love you, Issey, and the way that you carry on and on and on, from your centuries-old traditions, down through the ages, utilizing your total instinct and great integrity, to present artistry and beautiful inspirations that are so well applied to the present tense of East and West."

BELOW Guests at the show for S/S 1974.

OVERLEAF Models wearing Issey Miyake, for a special show with an "East meets West" theme, to celebrate the one-year anniversary of Studio 54 in New York in 1978.

In 1973, Miyake moved back to Paris, arriving shortly after fellow Japanese designer Kenzo Takada was making waves with his "Jungle Jap" clothes, which featured big proportions, bright colours and unexpected patterns, partly based on Japanese artistic traditions. That year, Miyake staged his first show in the French capital. His collections were sculptural and spectacular, and he quickly became known among a wave of influential avant-garde Japanese designers, including Rei Kawakubo and Yohji Yamamoto, who arrived in Paris around the same time and whose unique approaches challenged existing notions of clothing and had an outsized impact on Western dress.

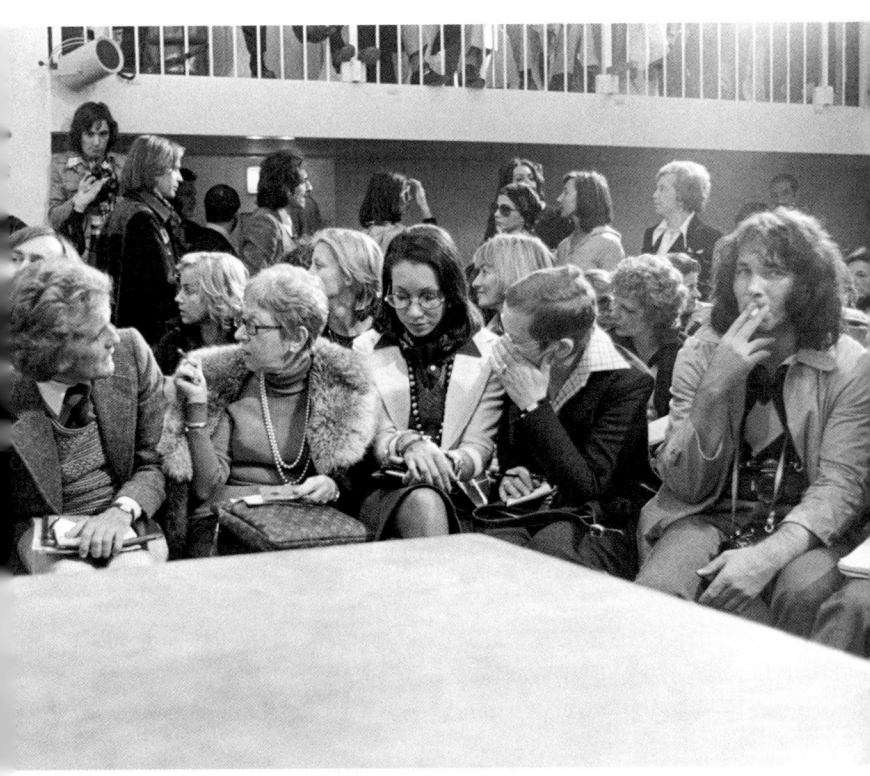

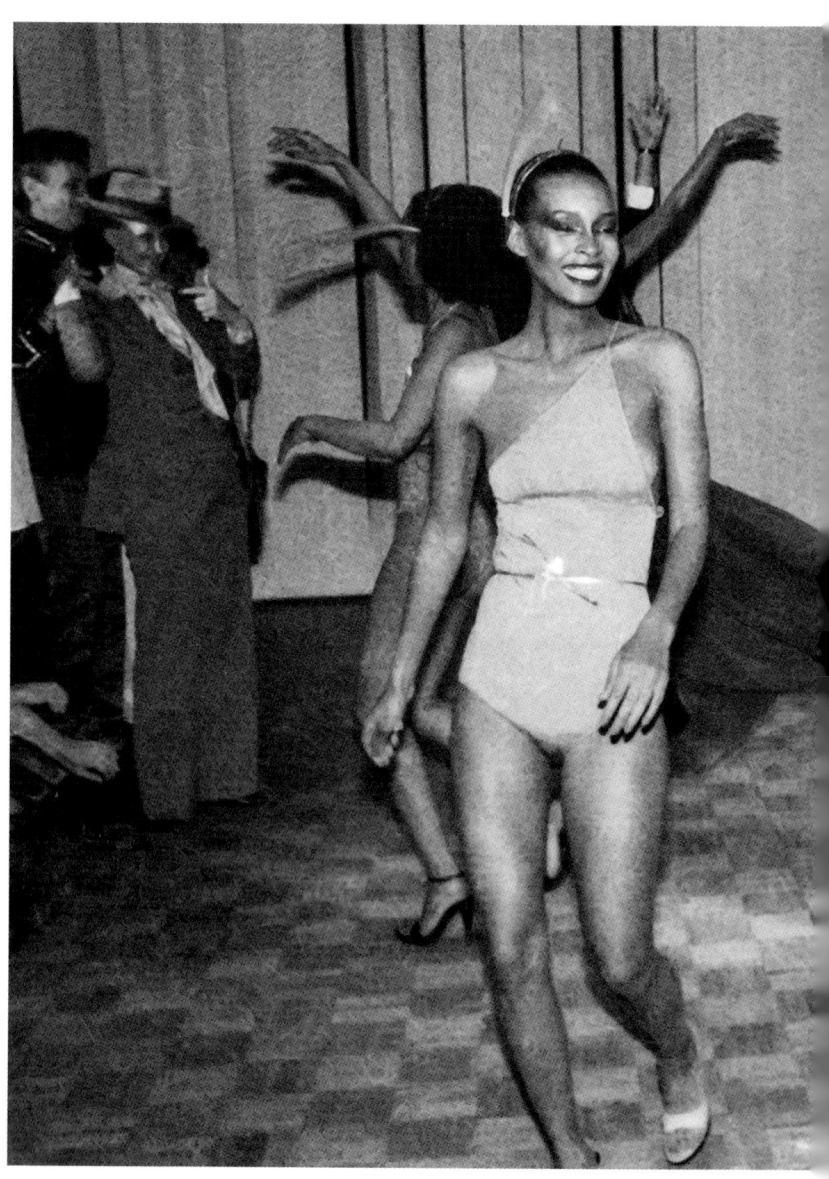

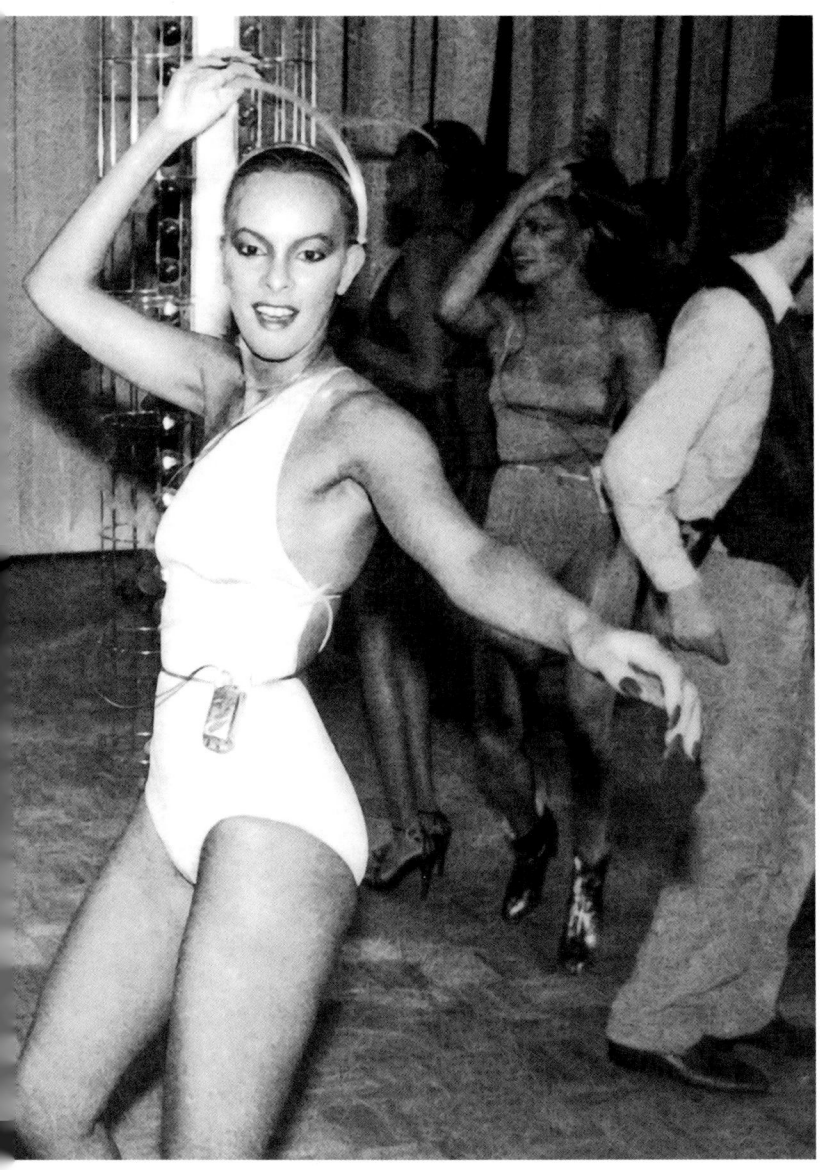

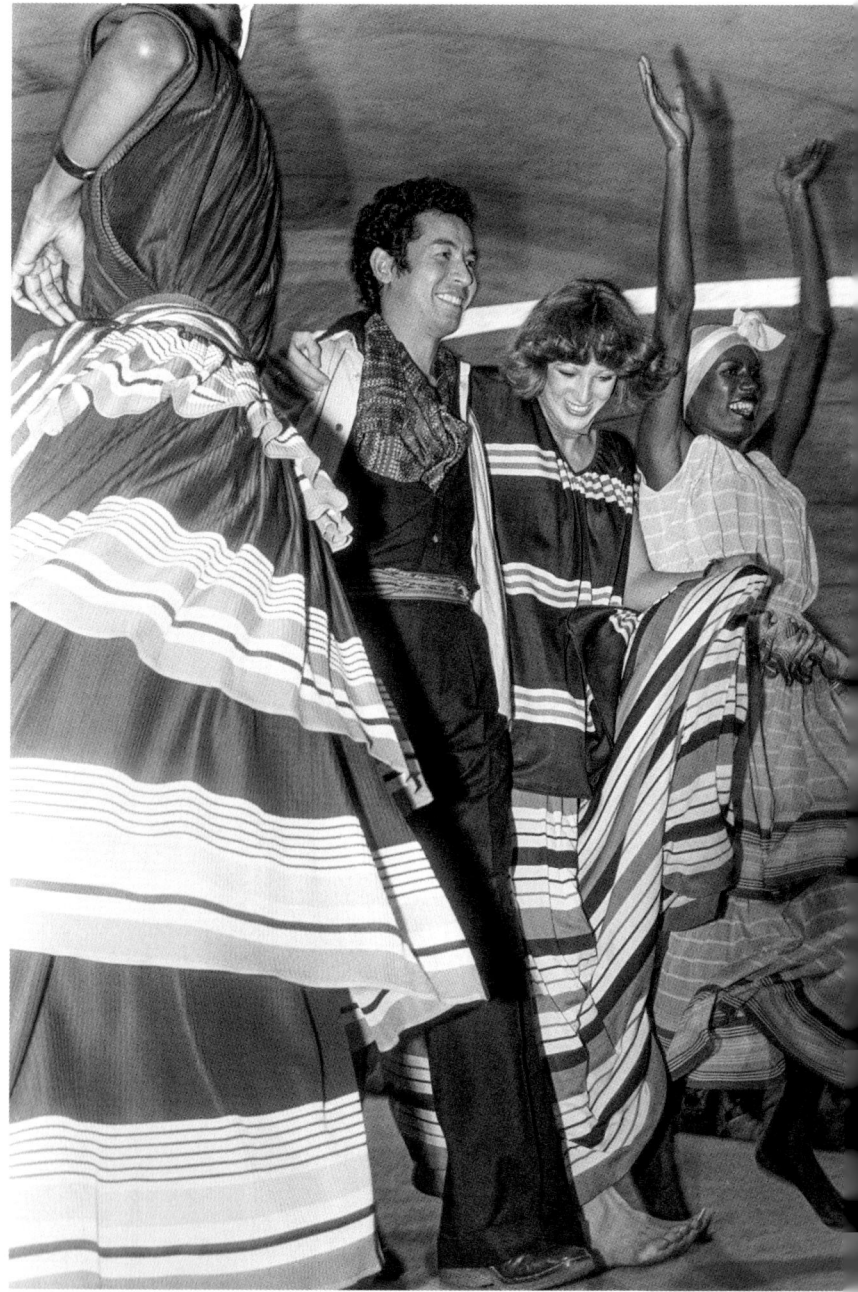

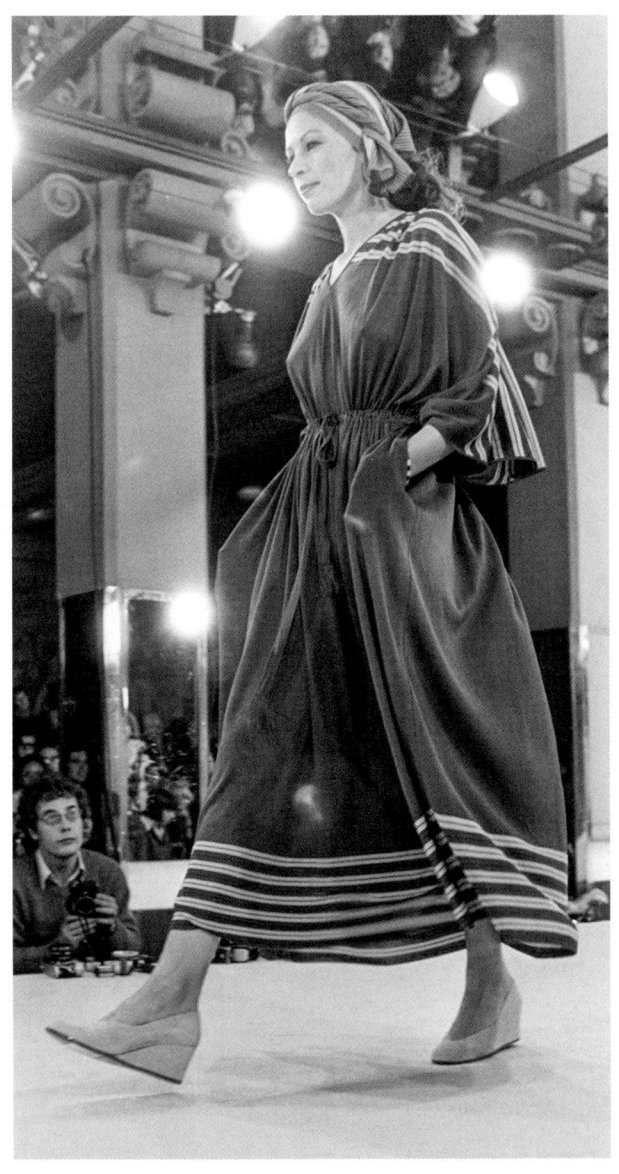

OPPOSITE Issey Miyake and models at his show for S/S 1976.

RIGHT A model walks for S/S 1975.

Like Kawakubo with Comme des Garçons and Yamamoto and his namesake label, Miyake's work is imbued with history while looking forward to the future. All three designers have commented over their careers that the kimono is the basis of their designs. Their unstructured and deconstructed garments acted as the antithesis of the fashion of the 1980s, which had been defined by exaggerated shoulder pads and body-clinging designs. They also worked differently to their European and American counterparts by dismissing popular cultural imagery and eschewing change for change's sake in favour of evolving and refining past research and collections.

RIGHT Issey Miyake and designer Kansai Yamamoto prepare for a joint fashion show at Tokyo's National Olympics Memorial Youth Center in 1974.

OPPOSITE From A/W 1977.

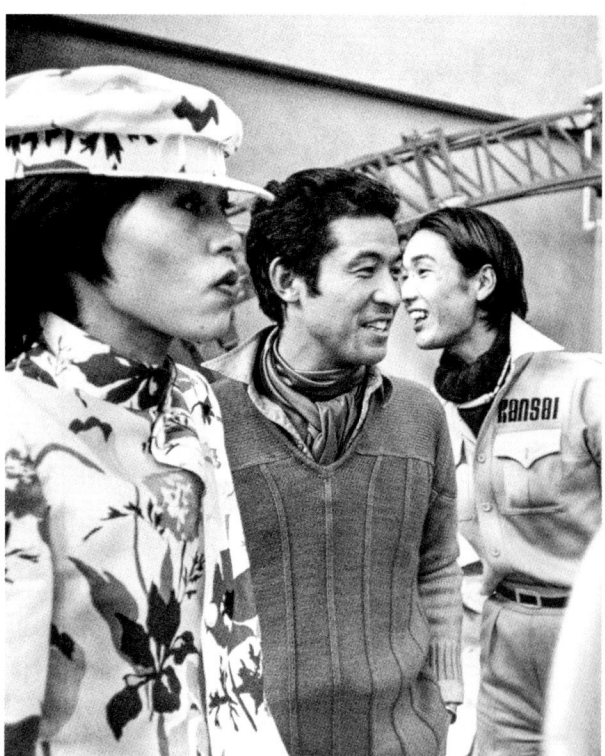

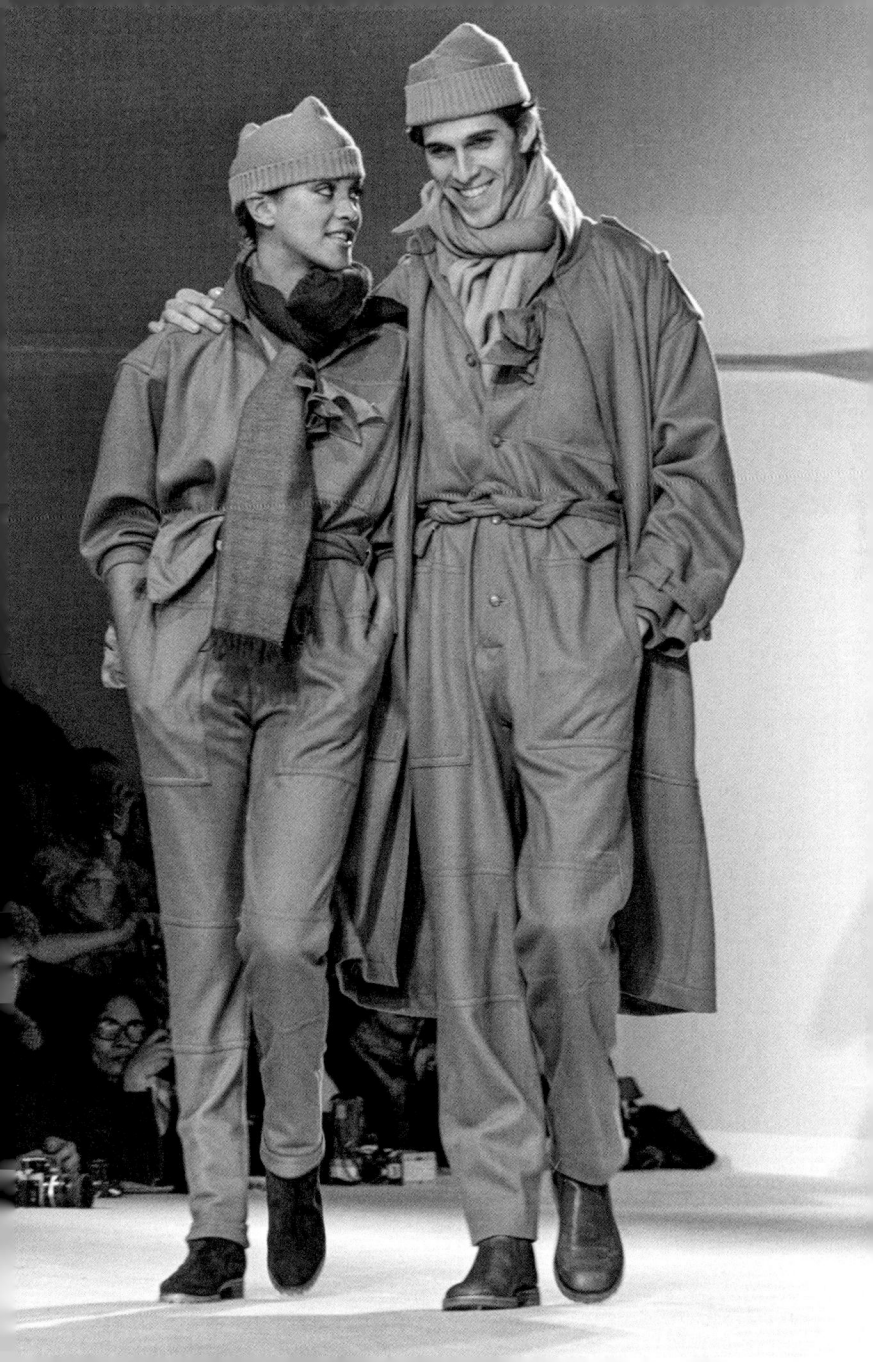

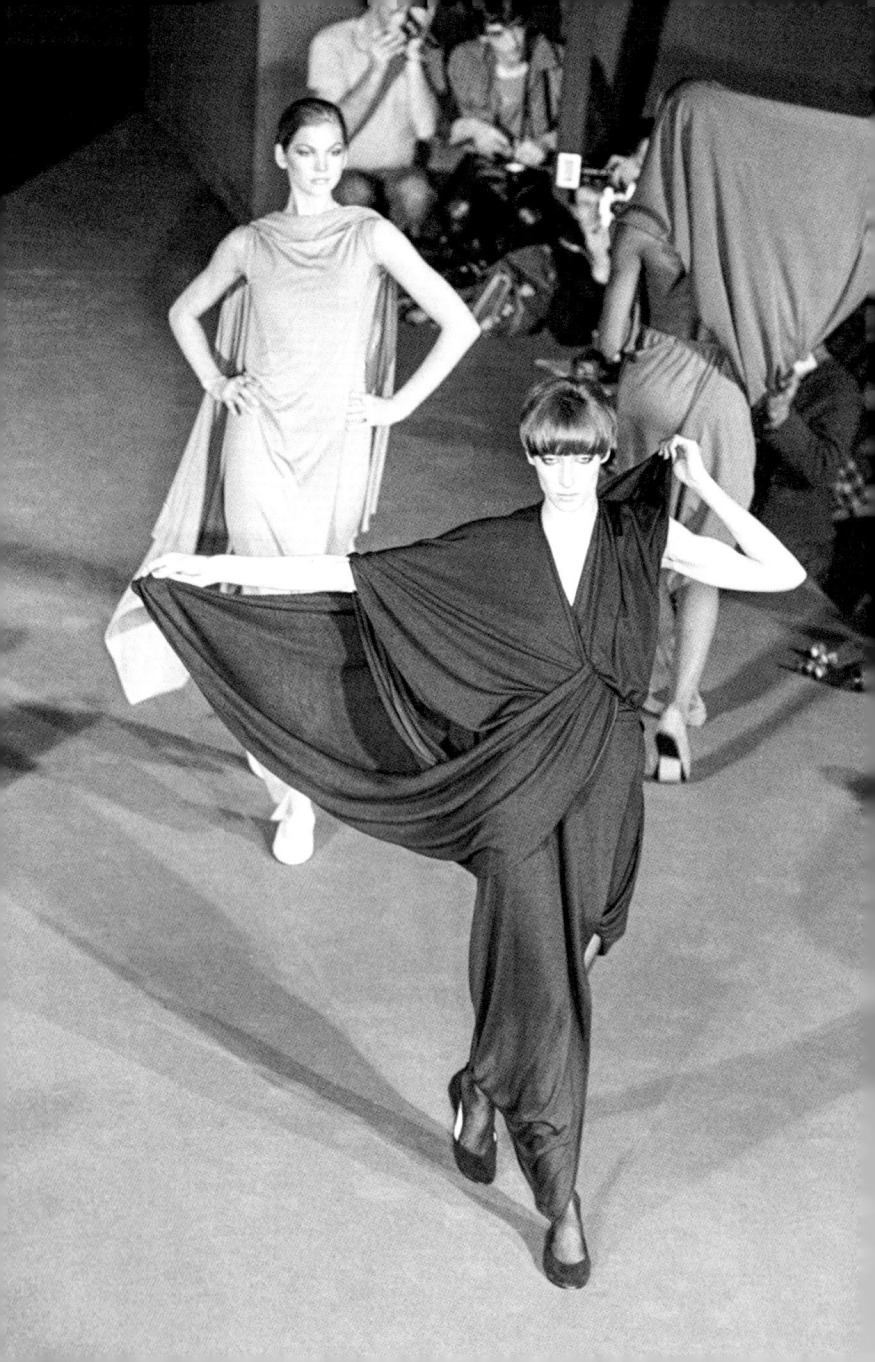

RIGHT A model
wearing designs for
S/S 1977.

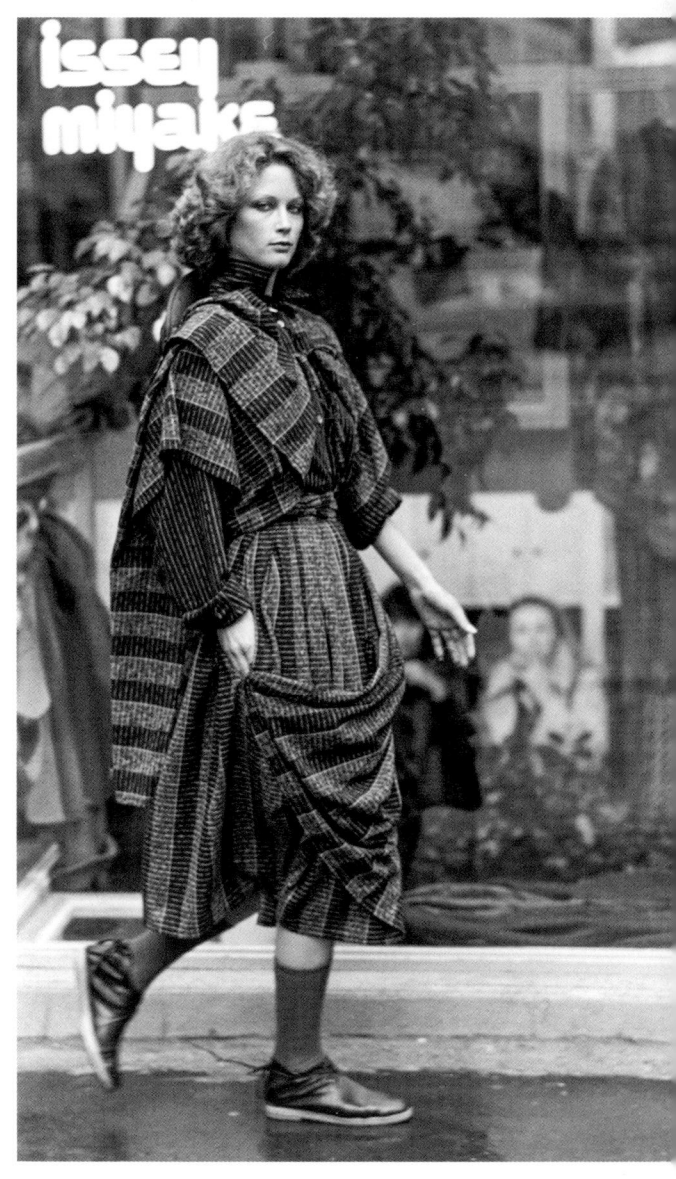

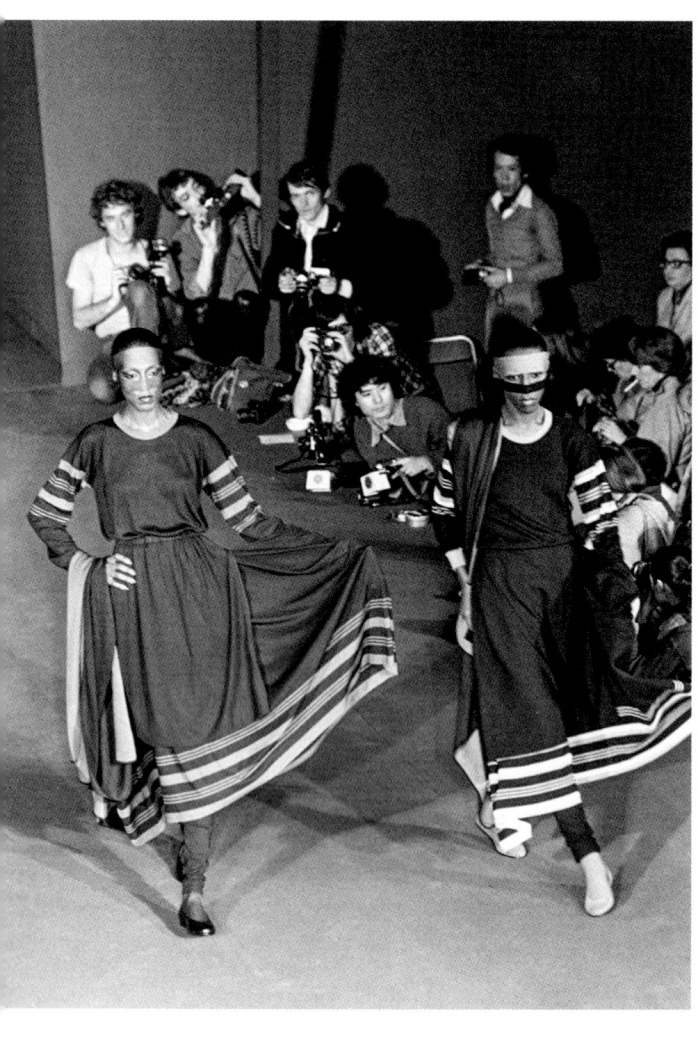

LEFT From A/W 1976.

OPPOSITE From S/S 1977.

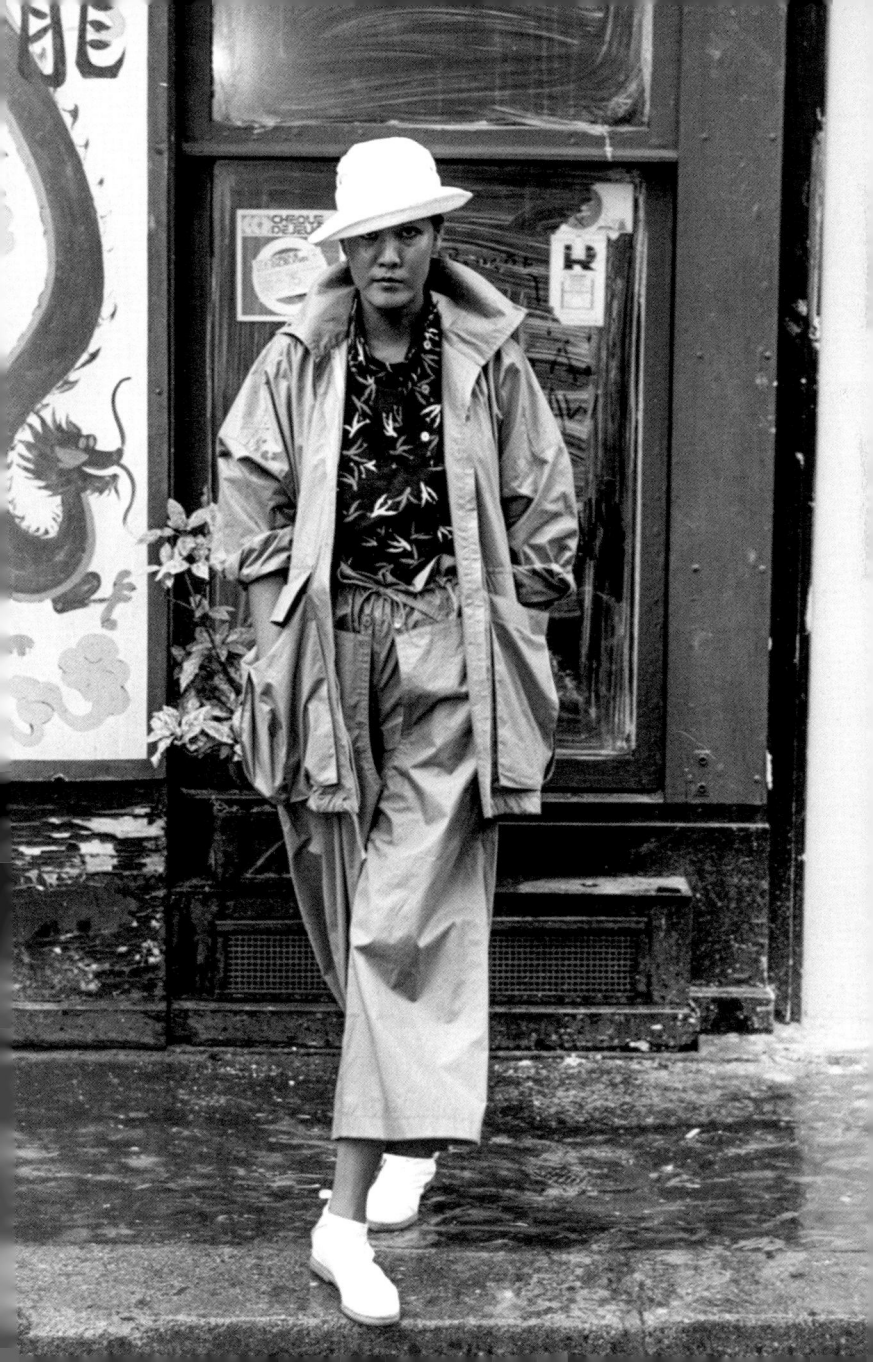

BELOW Models walk the show for S/S 1983, held on USS *Intrepid*, an aircraft carrier now moored at Pier 86, New York, where it serves as a museum.

OPPOSITE A model wearing a kimono jacket from S/S 1973.

There were also points of differentiation between Miyake and his peers. While the clothes of the impossibly cool Kawakubo and the poetic Yamamoto can impose upon the wearer, their designs more closely aligned with the esoteric world of haute couture, Miyake's designs are arguably more liberating. In a 1988 piece in prominent art magazine *Artforum*, editor Mark Holborn described how Miyake's unique approach "undermined our own Euro-centred perspective."

The Issey Miyake brand has continued to show in Paris, twice a year, ever since.

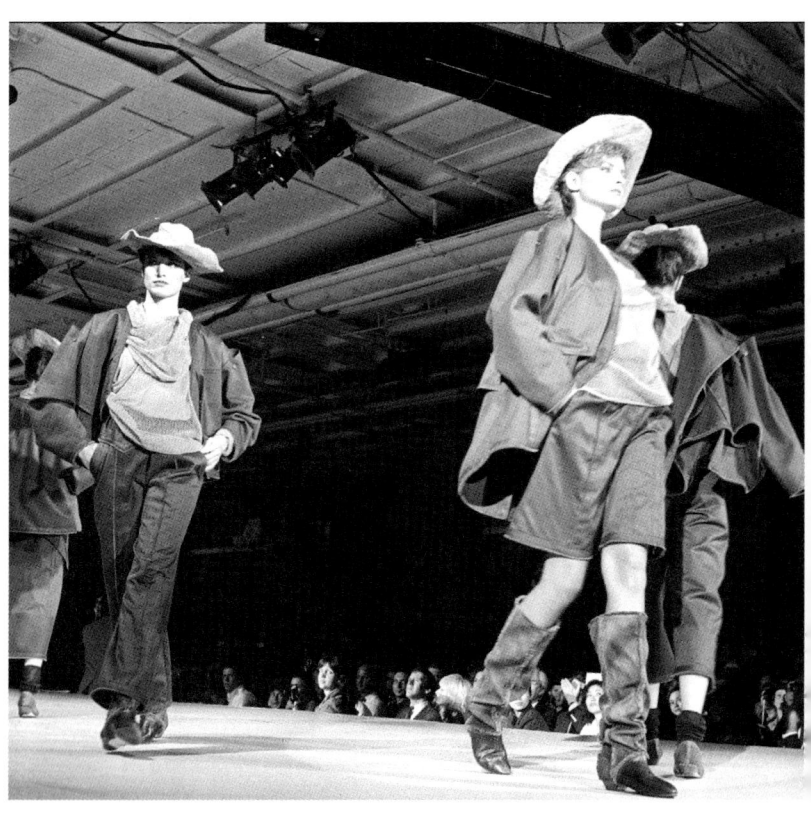

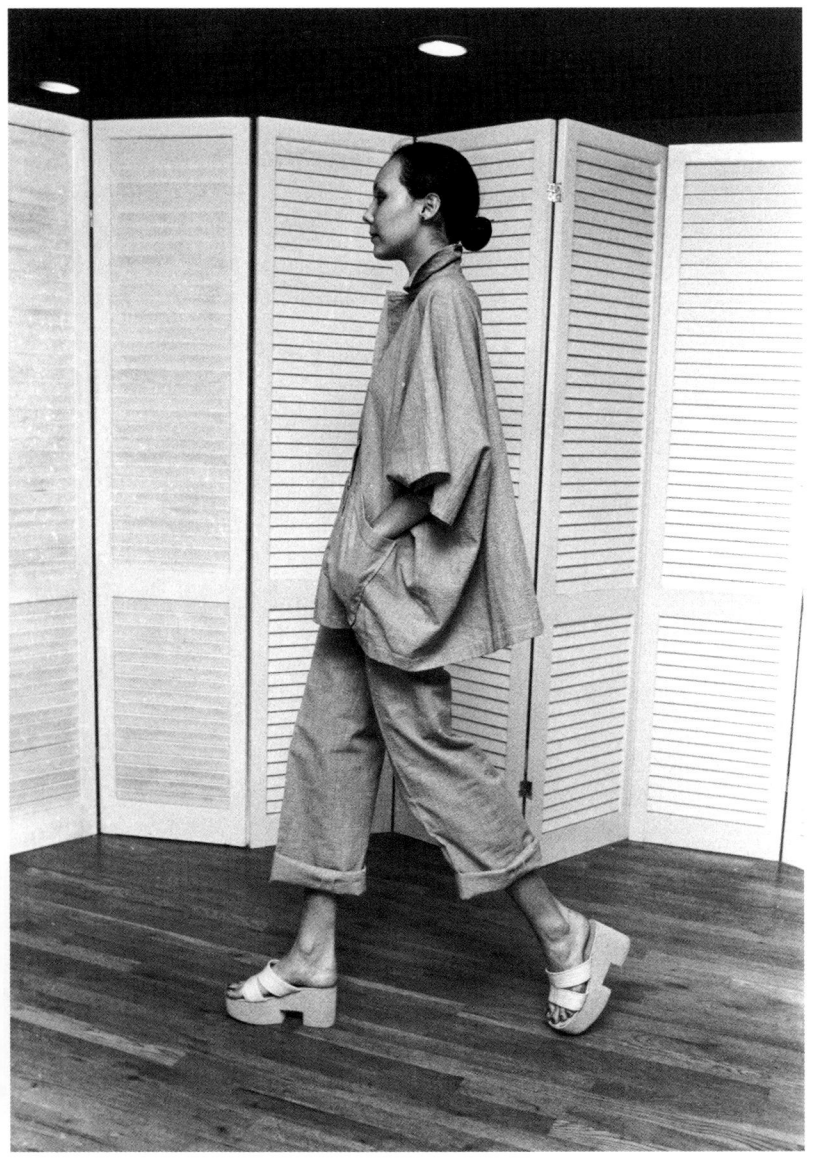

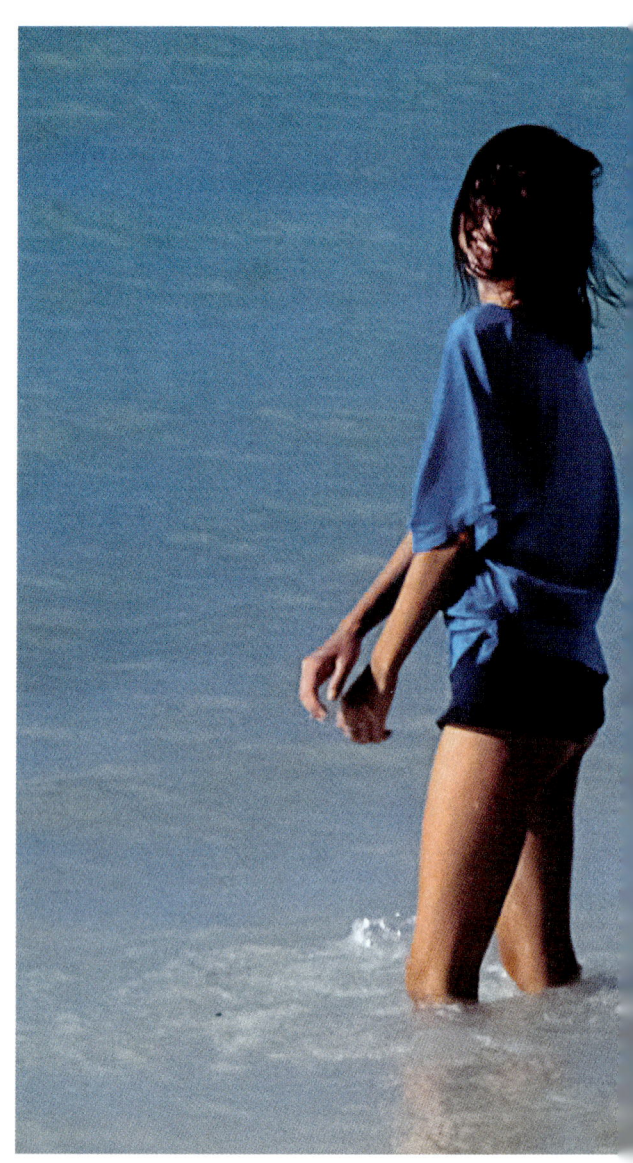

RIGHT Models in
the ocean wearing
Issey Miyake's blue
cotton beach tops
for *Vogue* in April
1977.

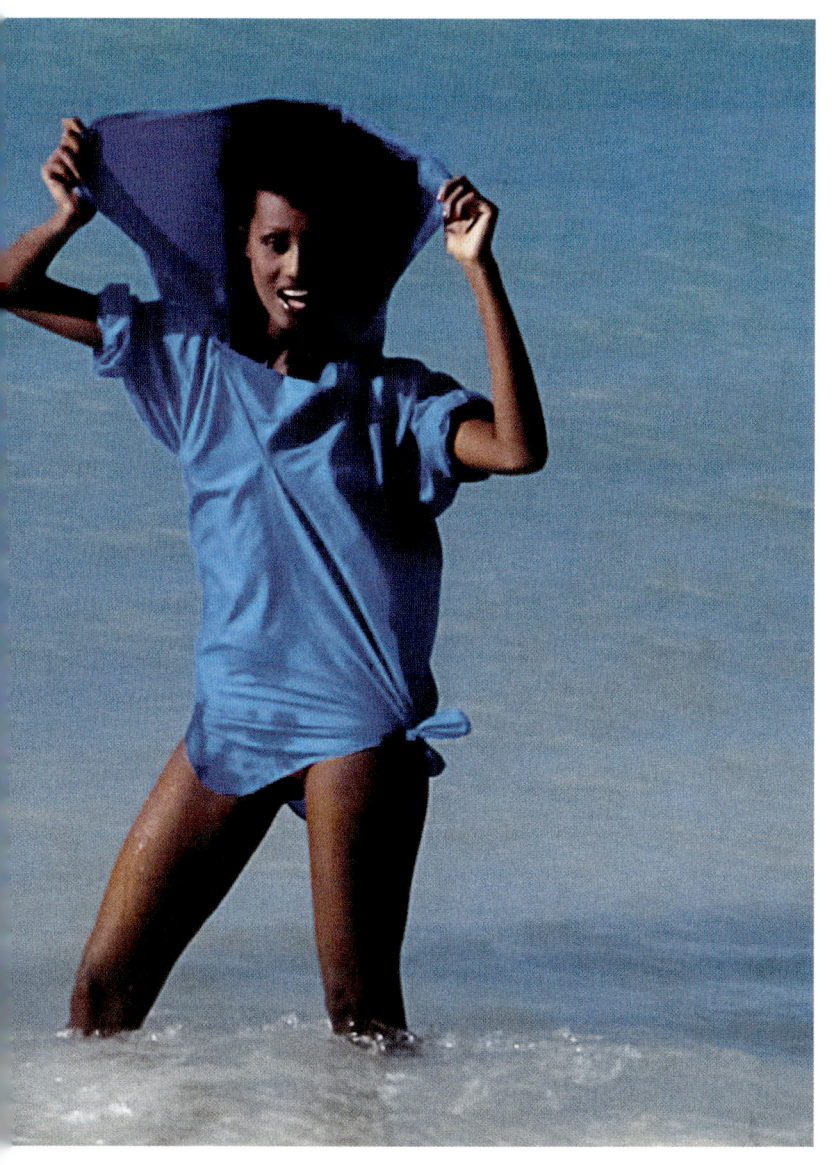

RISE TO
INTERNATIONAL
RECOGNITION

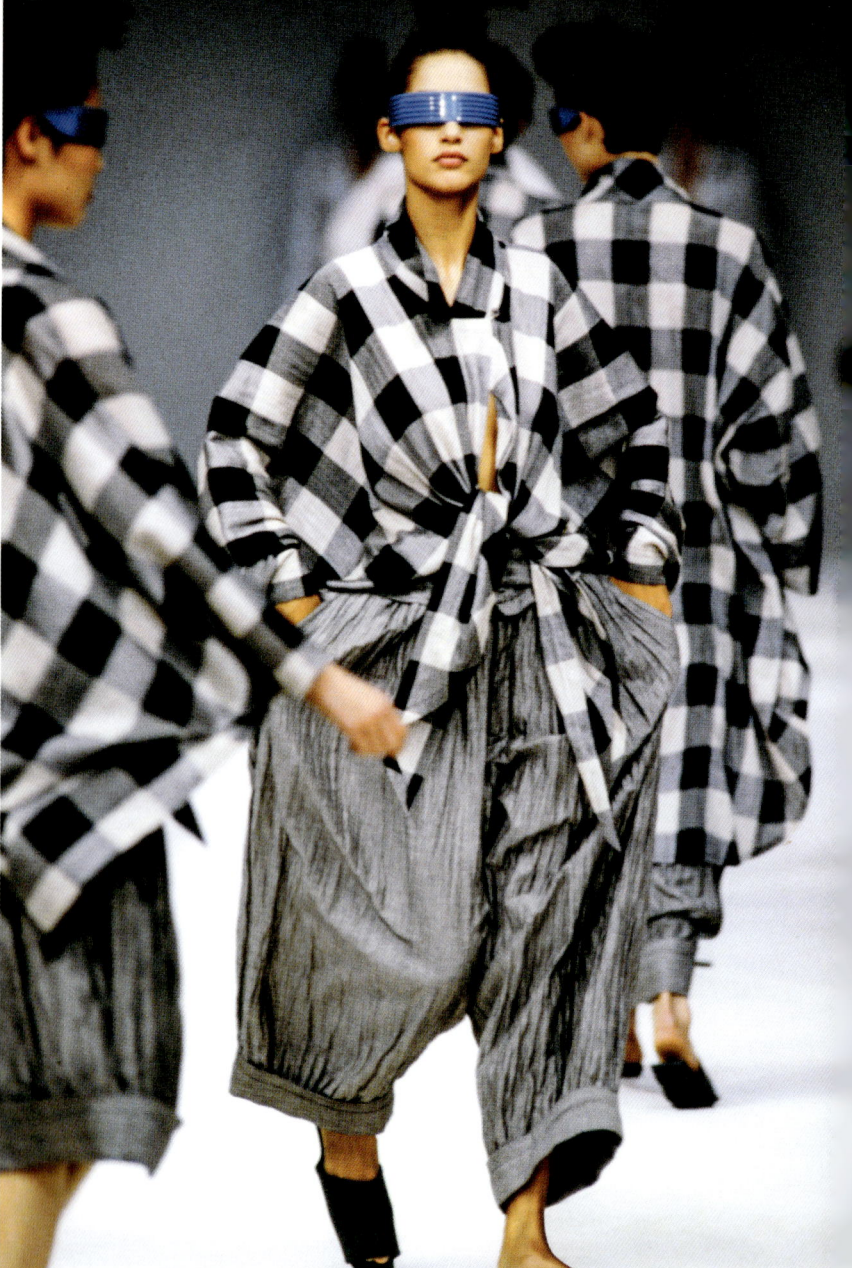

THE DESIGNER'S DESIGNER

Throughout the 80s, Miyake's network of stores grew.
The brand was gaining recognition worldwide and by 1983
it was generating $50 million in sales.

Miyake saw an opportunity to experiment with materials other than cloth and he created garments from plastic, paper and wire. In 1982, Miyake's gown made of rattan vines was the first piece of clothing shown on the cover of *Artforum*. Miyake also began integrating technology into his work, which led to the creation of new fabrics and forms, seen via his Body series, which included the famous bustiers made of plastic, rattan and resin. The unusual materials were used to reimagine the female body as a type of armour.

OPPOSITE From S/S 1986.

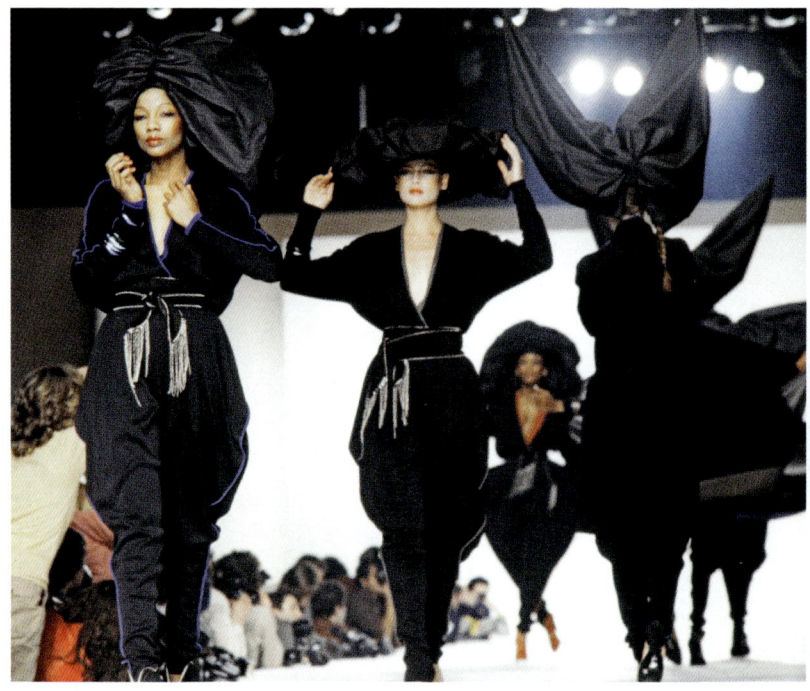

ABOVE Model
Mounia Orosemane
walks for A/W 1979,
shown in Paris.

OPPOSITE Grace
Jones performs at
London's Drury
Lane Theatre in
1981, wearing a
bustier designed by
Issey Miyake.

Miyake continued to draw attention around the world as he put on two major exhibitions: "Issey Miyake Spectacle: Bodyworks", which featured the famous bustier and toured internationally across Tokyo, Los Angeles, San Francisco and London from 1983 to 1985; and "Issey Miyake A-Un", held in 1988 at the Musée des Arts Décoratifs in Paris and consisting of the research and materials behind 76 outfits that Miyake and his colleague Makiko Minagawa had worked on over the past year. These included oiled paper – traditionally used for Japanese umbrellas – that had been softened by hand and corrugated fabric made up of multiple layers of compressed wool.

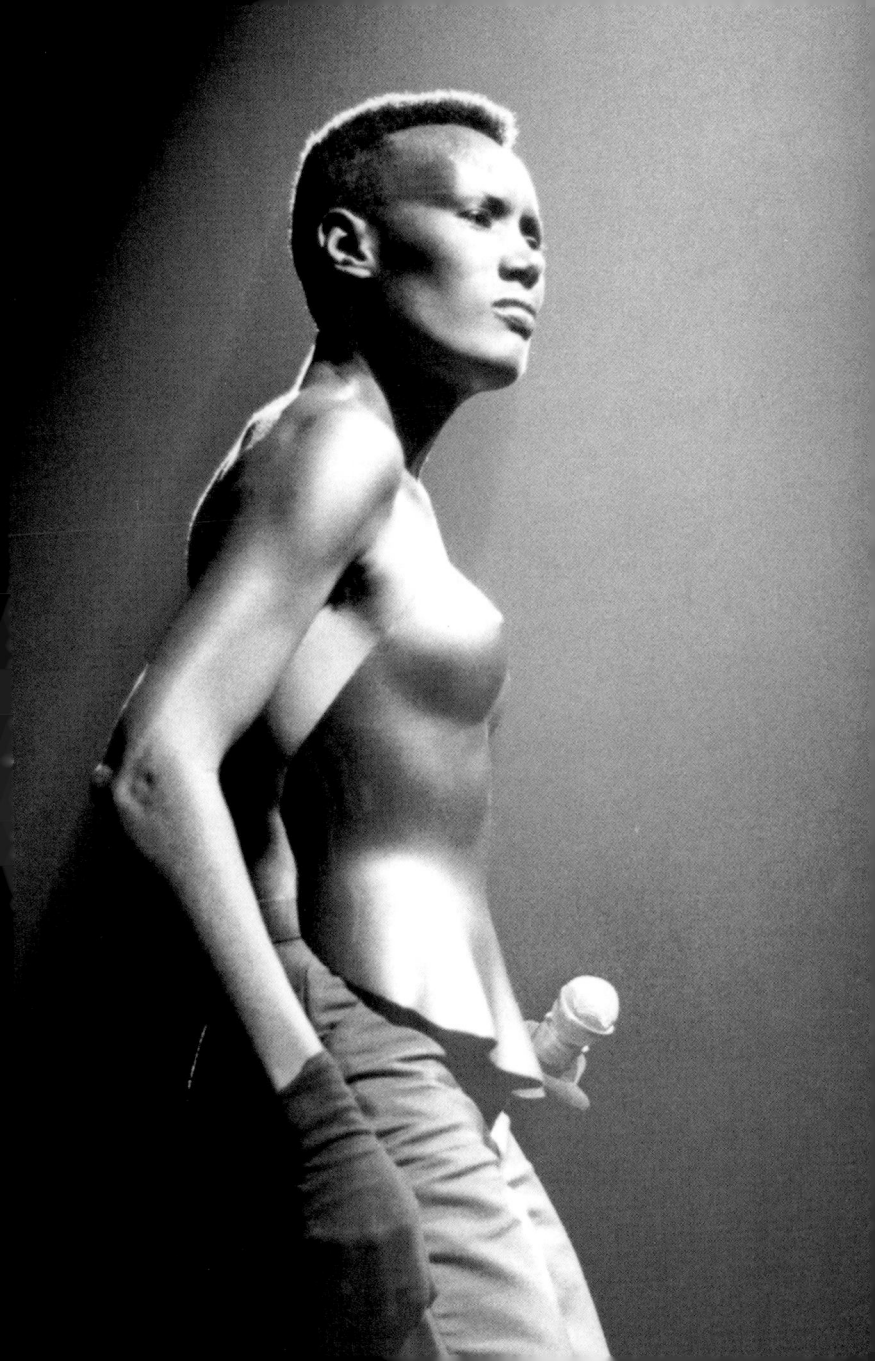

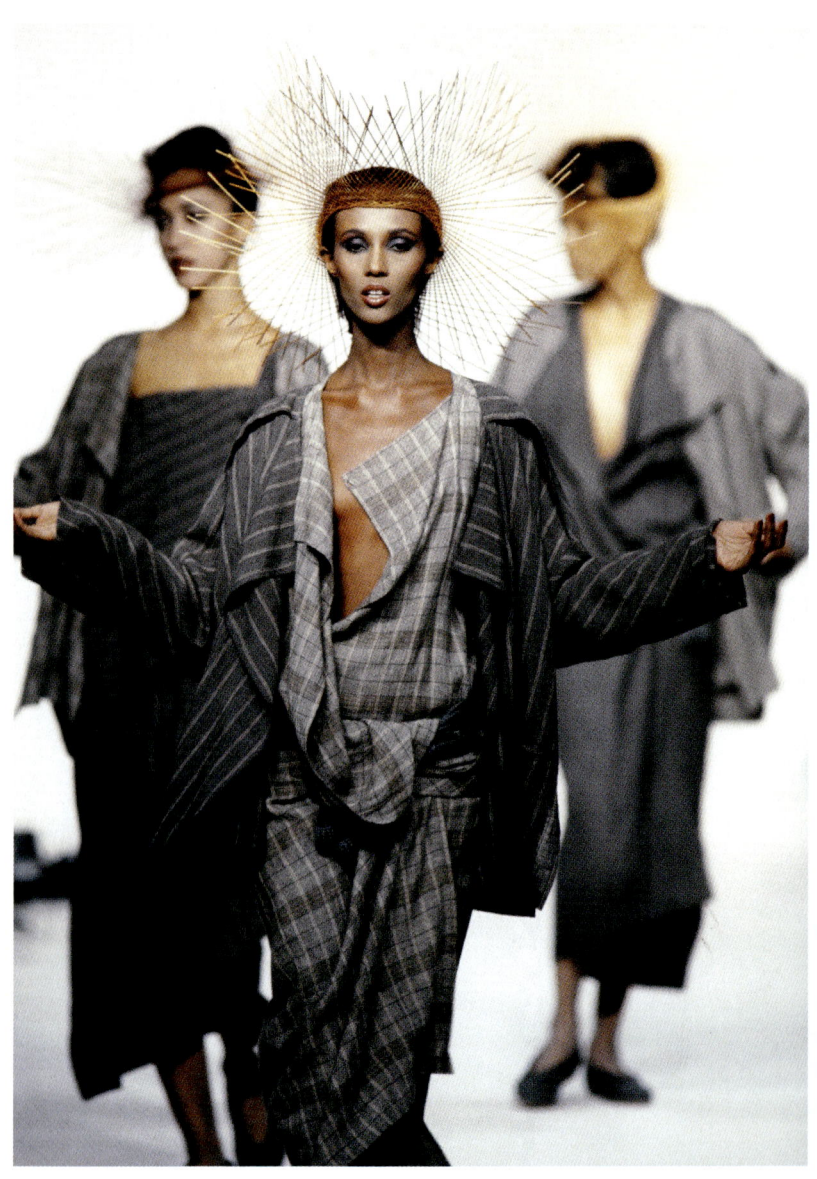

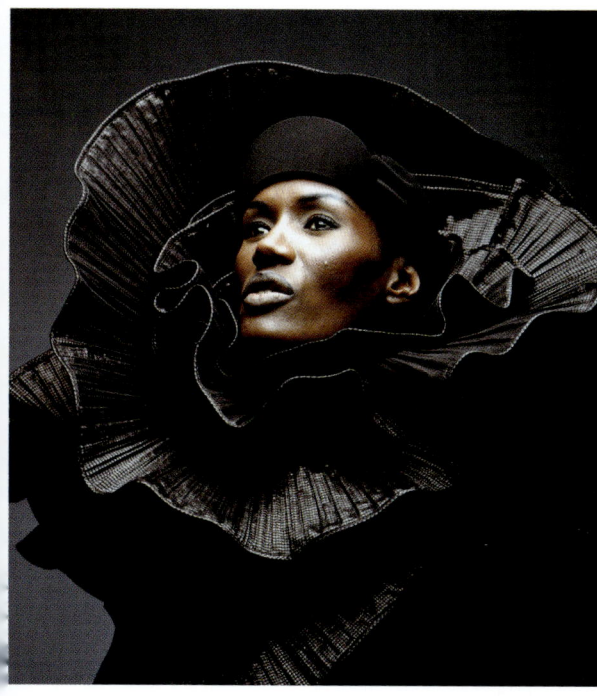

In 1986, Miyake's clothing appeared on the cover of *Time* magazine (January 27), accompanied by the article "Changing Clothes: Issey Miyake", which delved into his approach to design and attitude to life.

A key proponent of Miyake's philosophy was about thinking beyond trends and instead prioritizing the needs of society. In 1976, Miyake cast singer-songwriter and model Grace Jones (who would continue to be a longstanding collaborator throughout his career) in one of his defining fashion shows, *Issey Miyake and Twelve Black Girls*. This was radical and empowering at a time when the European modelling industry lacked diversity.

Miyake's democratic approach continued into the 1980s when he cast models who were only around 1.72m (5ft 8in), unlike the towering women on the runways of that era, such as Iman and Jerry Hall. And this was a decade before the waifish 1.7m (5ft 7in) Kate Moss arrived on the scene. In 1996, Miyake cast six women over the age of 60 to walk in his runway show at the Carrousel du Louvre, including a psychiatrist spotted by his assistant at a Japanese restaurant.

Miyake was a pioneer of collaborations, particularly those that blended fashion with art, and it was through this spirit that he was willing to have a public profile. "The worst thing about the 1980s is that designers became stars," Miyake told *Holborn* in 1995. "Design is not an extension of my ego. Design is teamwork. I employ many people. Design carries great responsibility."

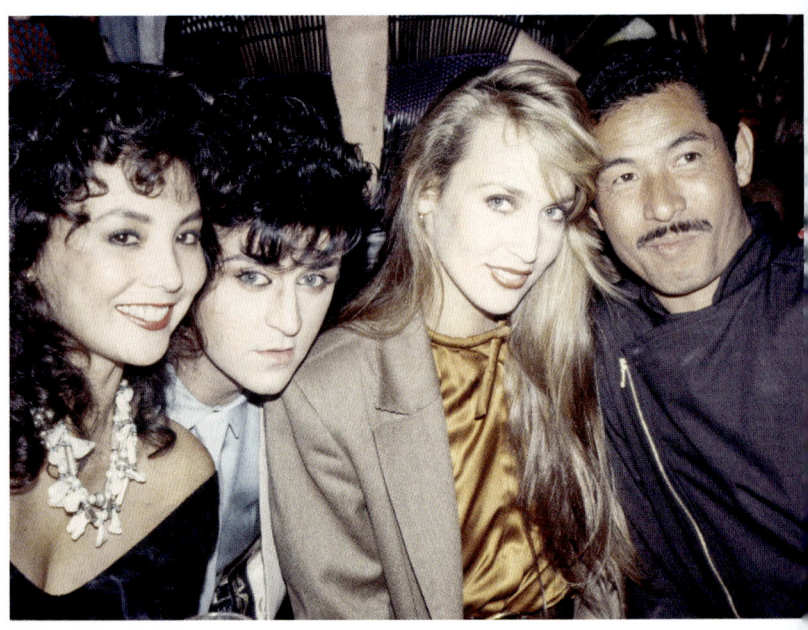

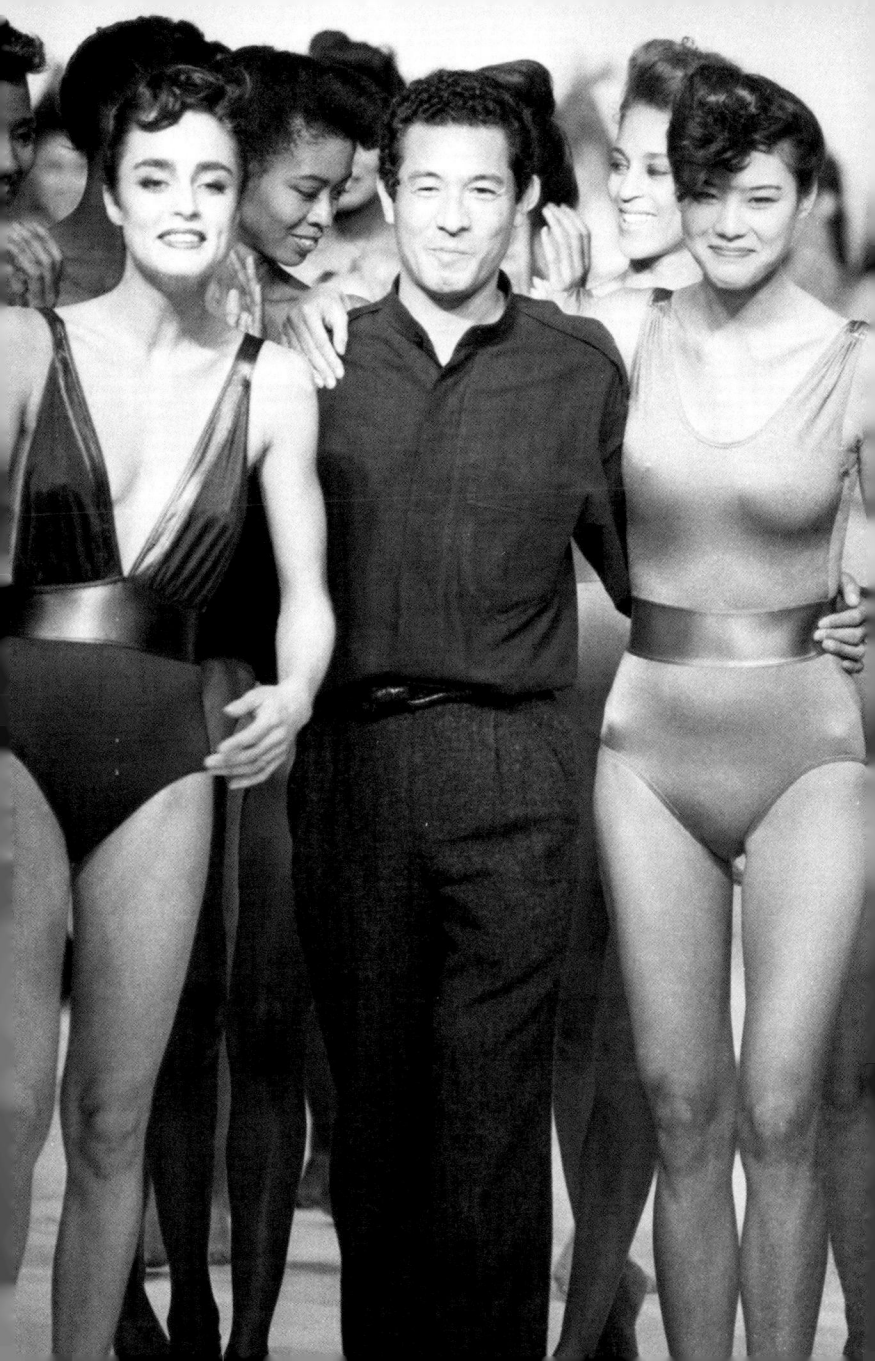

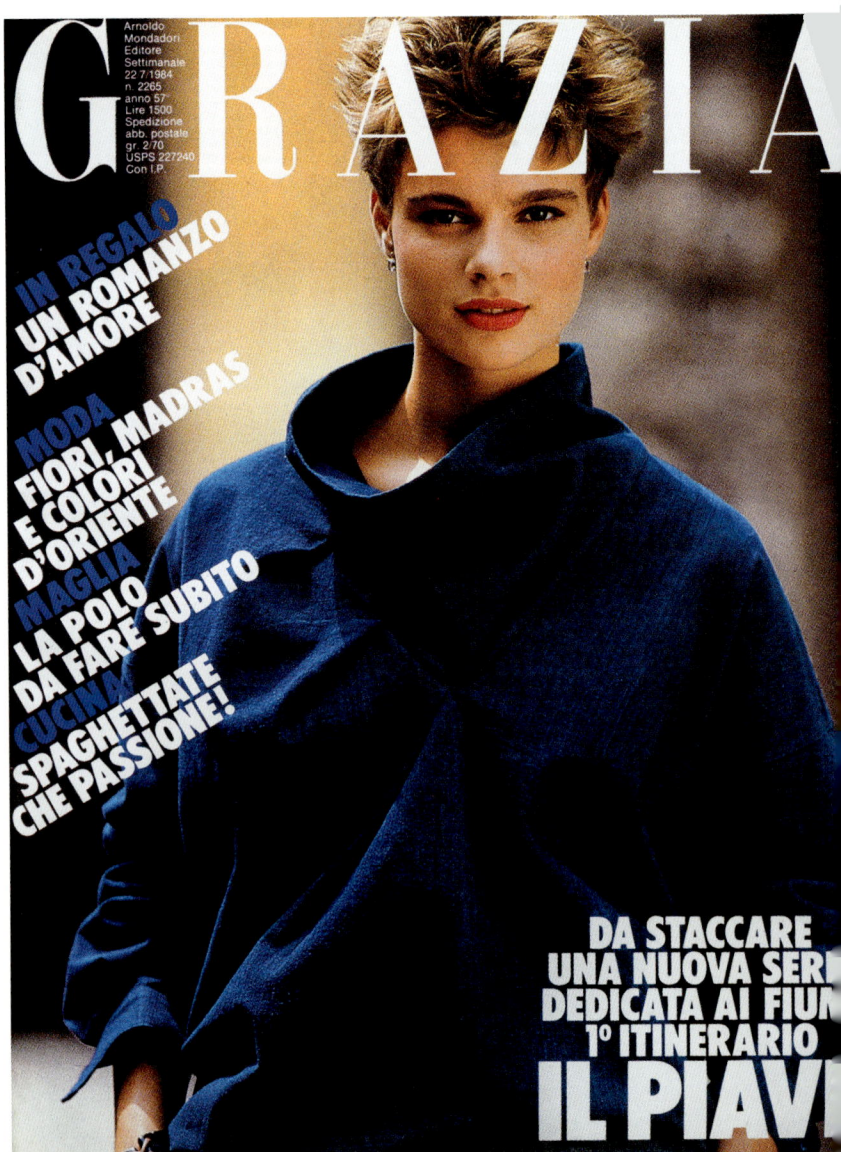

Arnoldo
Mondadori
Editore
Settimanale
22 7/1984
n. 2265
anno 57
Lire 1500
Spedizione
abb. postale
gr. 2/70
USPS 227240
Con I.P.

GRAZIA

IN REGALO
UN ROMANZO
D'AMORE

MODA
FIORI, MADRAS
E COLORI
D'ORIENTE

MAGLIA
LA POLO
DA FARE SUBITO

CUCINA
SPAGHETTATE
CHE PASSIONE!

DA STACCARE
UNA NUOVA SERI
DEDICATA AI FIUM
1º ITINERARIO
IL PIAV

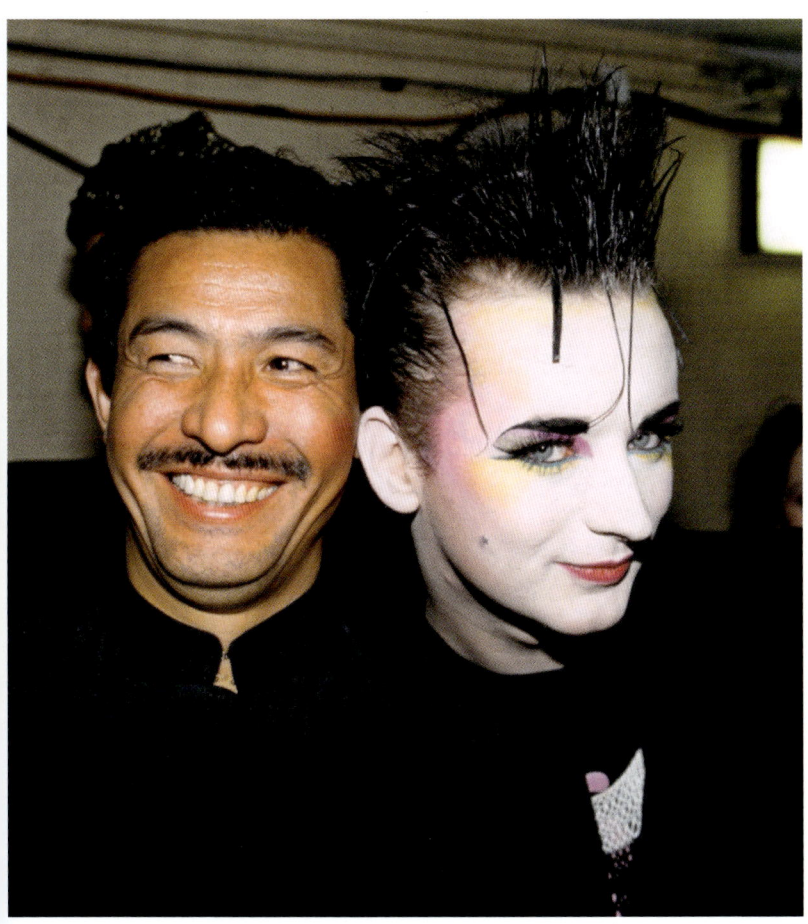

ABOVE Issey Miyake and singer Boy George at the
Fashion Aid charity fundraiser at London's Royal Albert
Hall in 1985.

OPPOSITE A model wearing an Issey Miyake sweater on
the cover of *Grazia* magazine, 1984.

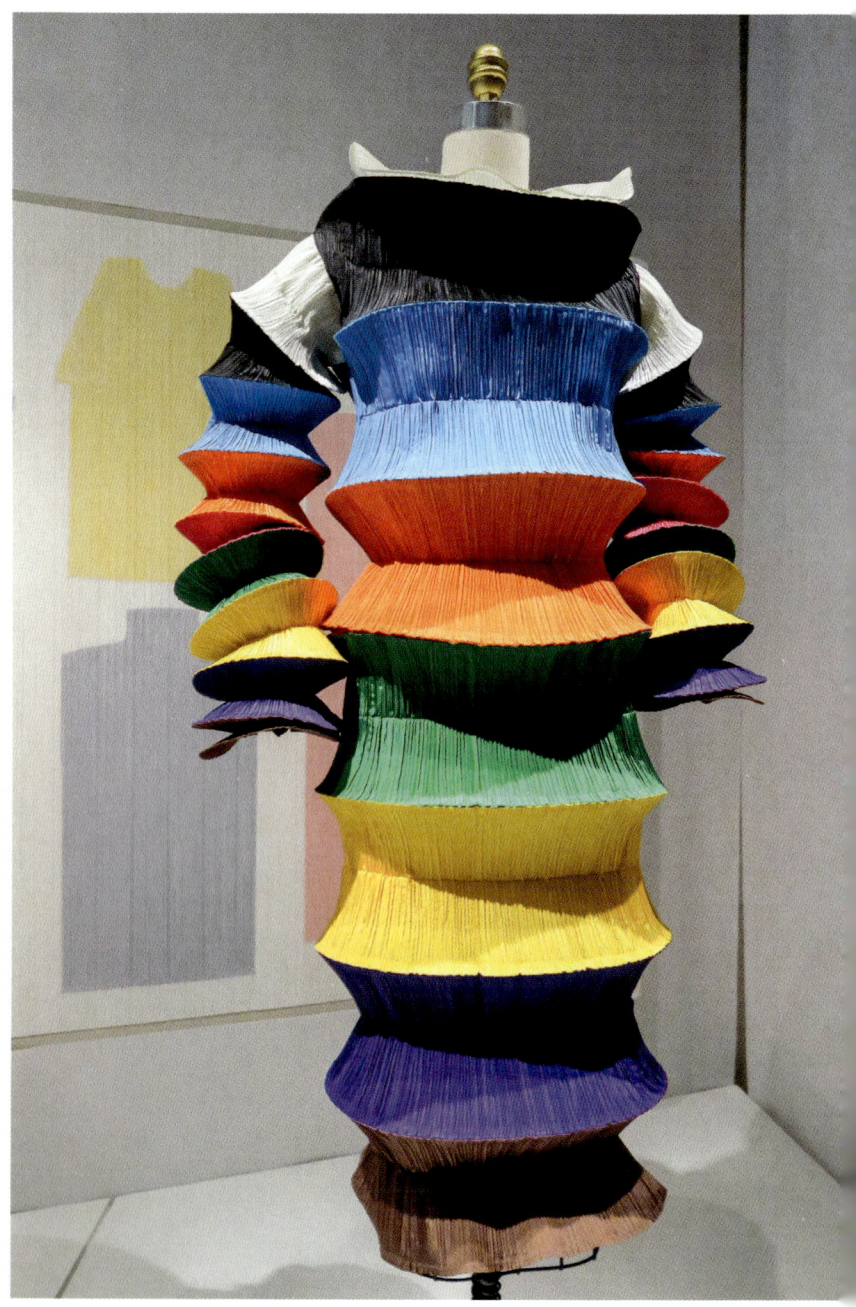

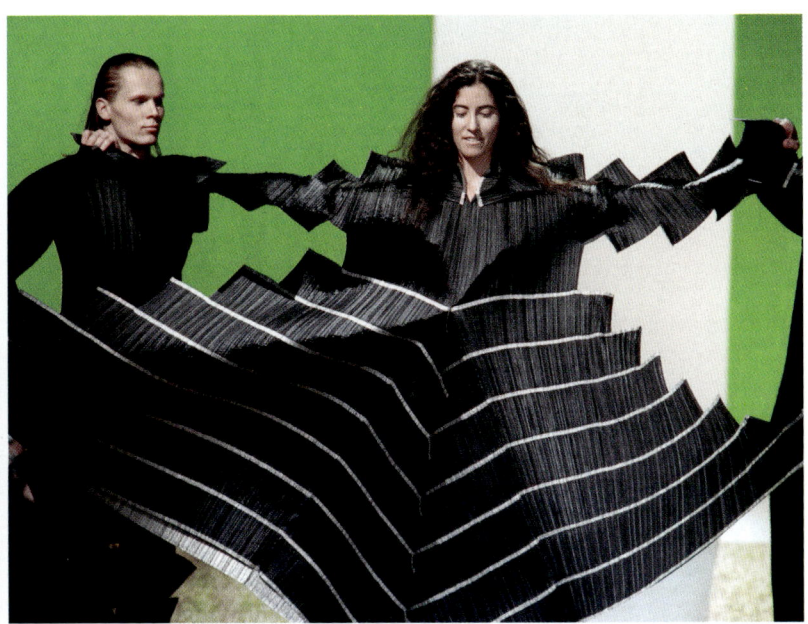

ABOVE The "Staircase" dress from A/W 1995.

OPPOSITE Issey Miyake's "Flying Saucer" dress, from S/S 1994, on display at the "Manus × Machina: Fashion in an Age of Technology" exhibition at the Metropolitan Museum of Art in New York.

One of his most notable collaborators was the photographer Irving Penn. The two began an unusually long-distance relationship in the 1980s when Penn first photographed the designer's pieces for *Vogue*. Every year Miyake would send his annual collections to Penn to be photographed. For Miyake, it was inspirational to see his creations through Penn's eyes, but he never went to the photoshoots, which all took place in Penn's studio in New York.

Models posed against a white background, wearing clothing that was, in some cases, straightforward and, in others, expanded in stratospheric ways – such as Miyake's "Flying Saucer" dress. Using the vocabulary of pleats that he introduced in the 90s, it was made of colourful weightless discs that could be compressed or extended.

OPPOSITE
A model wears
a multicoloured,
pleated look from
S/S 1993.

OVERLEAF From
A/W 1982.

Other still life photography by Penn shows Miyake's garments twisted or laid flat. Photos by Penn for "Twist", the 1992 Issey Miyake exhibition held at the Naoshima Contemporary Art Museum, feature twisted materials that were first inserted into a kiln for heat processing and then unfurled to become an item of clothing, such as a tank top, shirt, trousers or dress, with its own unique and random wrinkles. The idea was to create handmade and asymmetrical pleats, rather than orderly machine pleats.

"The reason I went to him [Penn] was the precision of his way of looking. He brings a very clear personal vision to everything he photographs," said Miyake, discussing the exhibition "Making Things". "His technique, which is extremely lucid, always delivers to us what he is thinking. That inspires me to really move forward. Penn helps me to find myself again, as if he was saying to me, 'Go back to your work.' Without him, I would quite likely not have continued to work all this time."

Both creatives also shared a common feeling for simplification and a love for nature. Seven books and a series of exhibitions were the fruits of their creative relationship across 13 years.

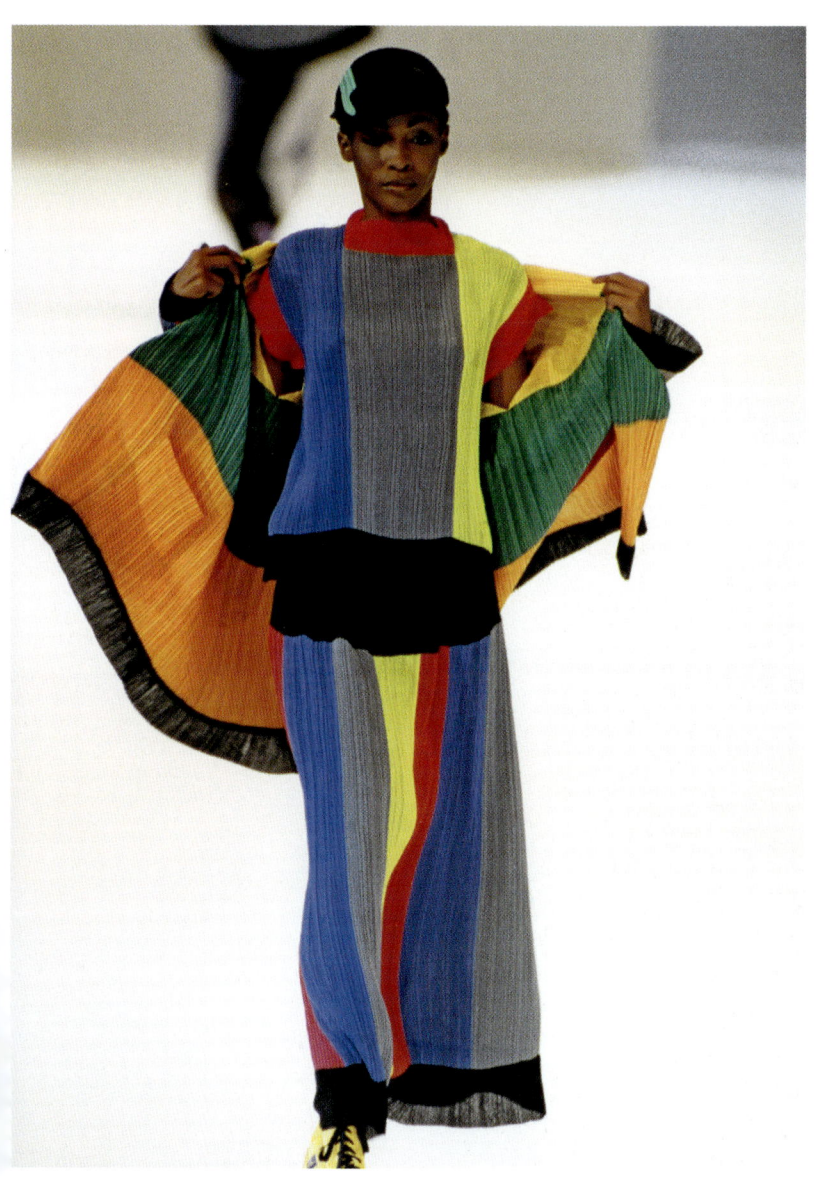

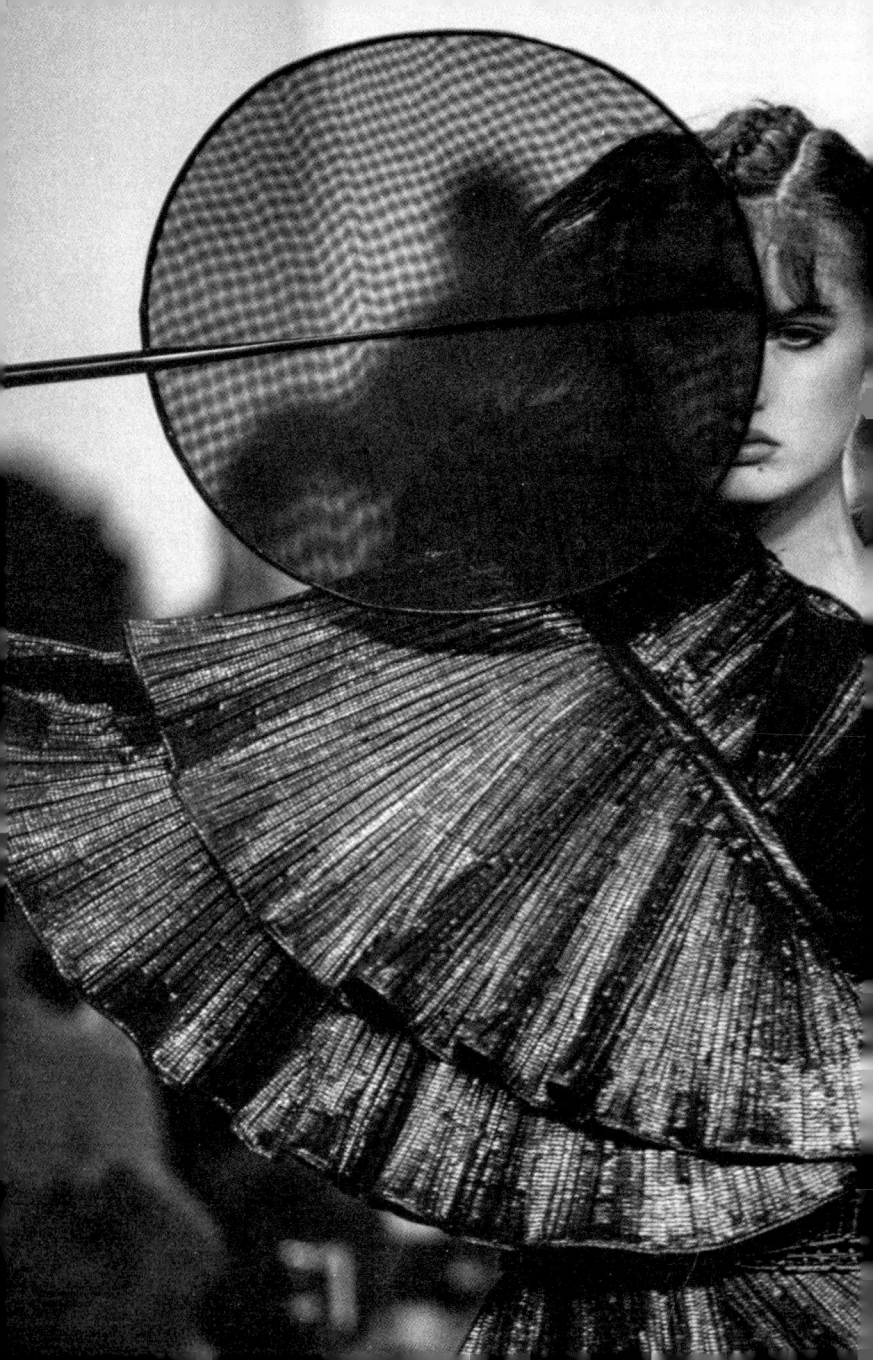

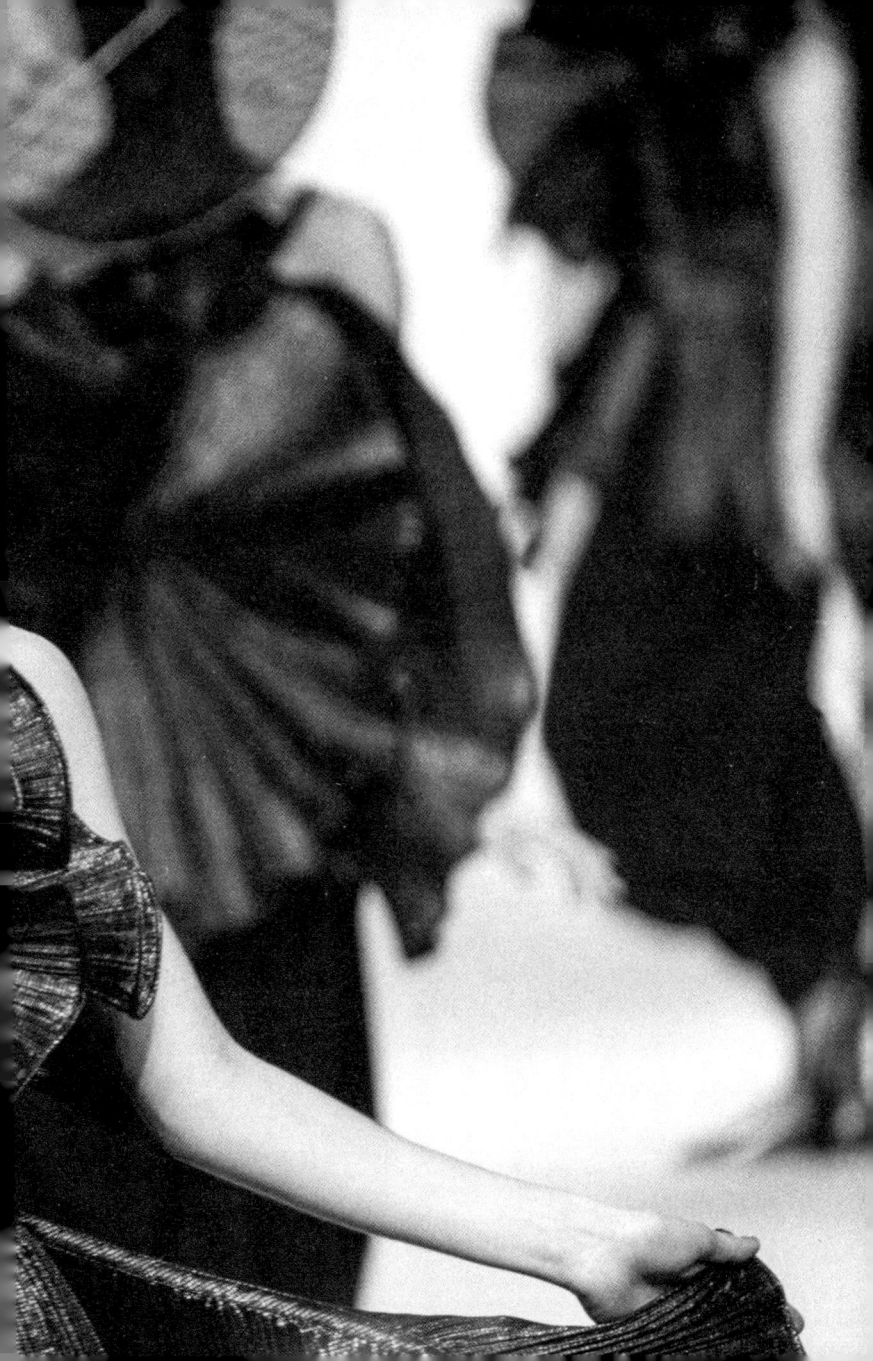

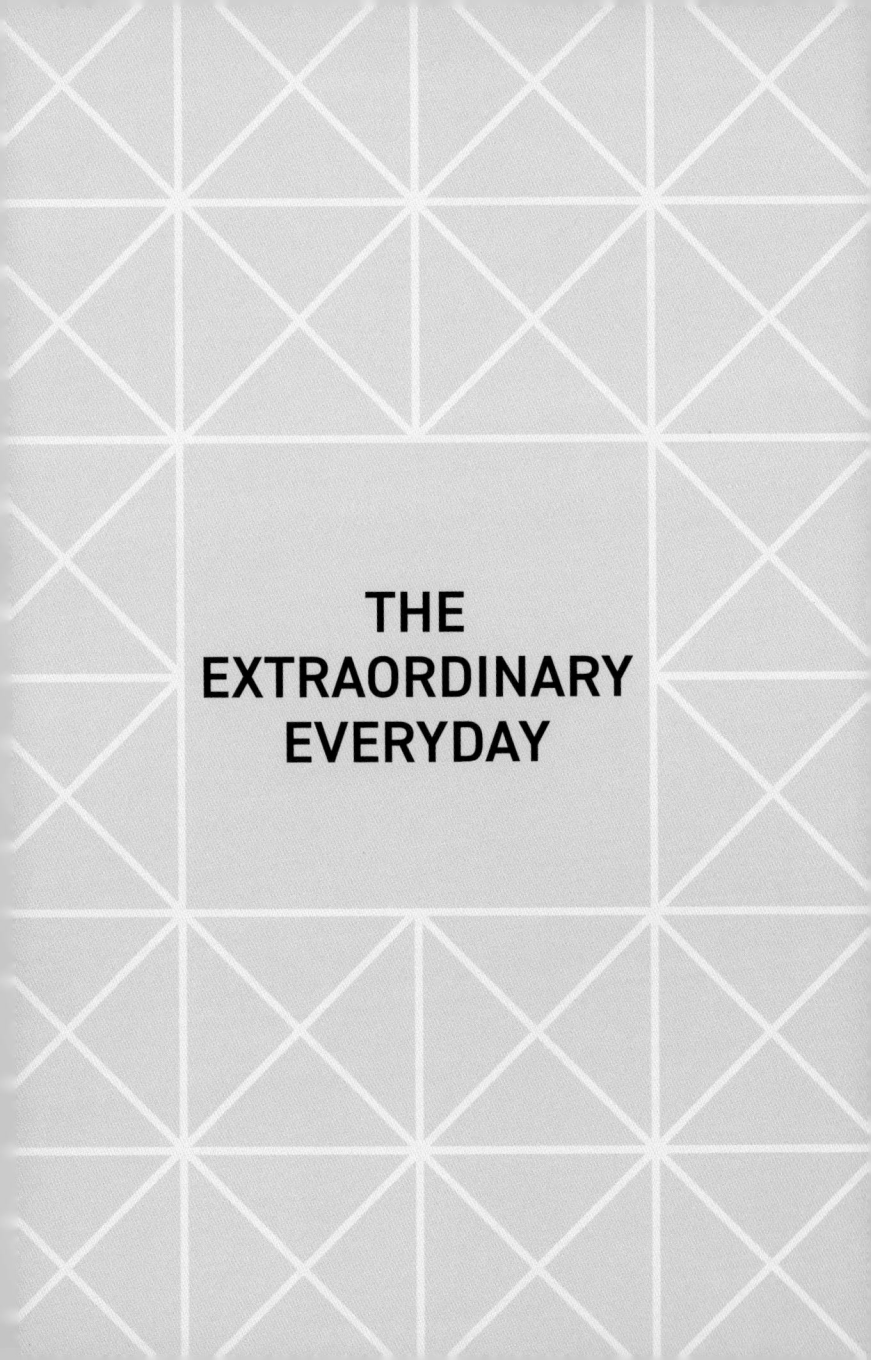

THE
EXTRAORDINARY
EVERYDAY

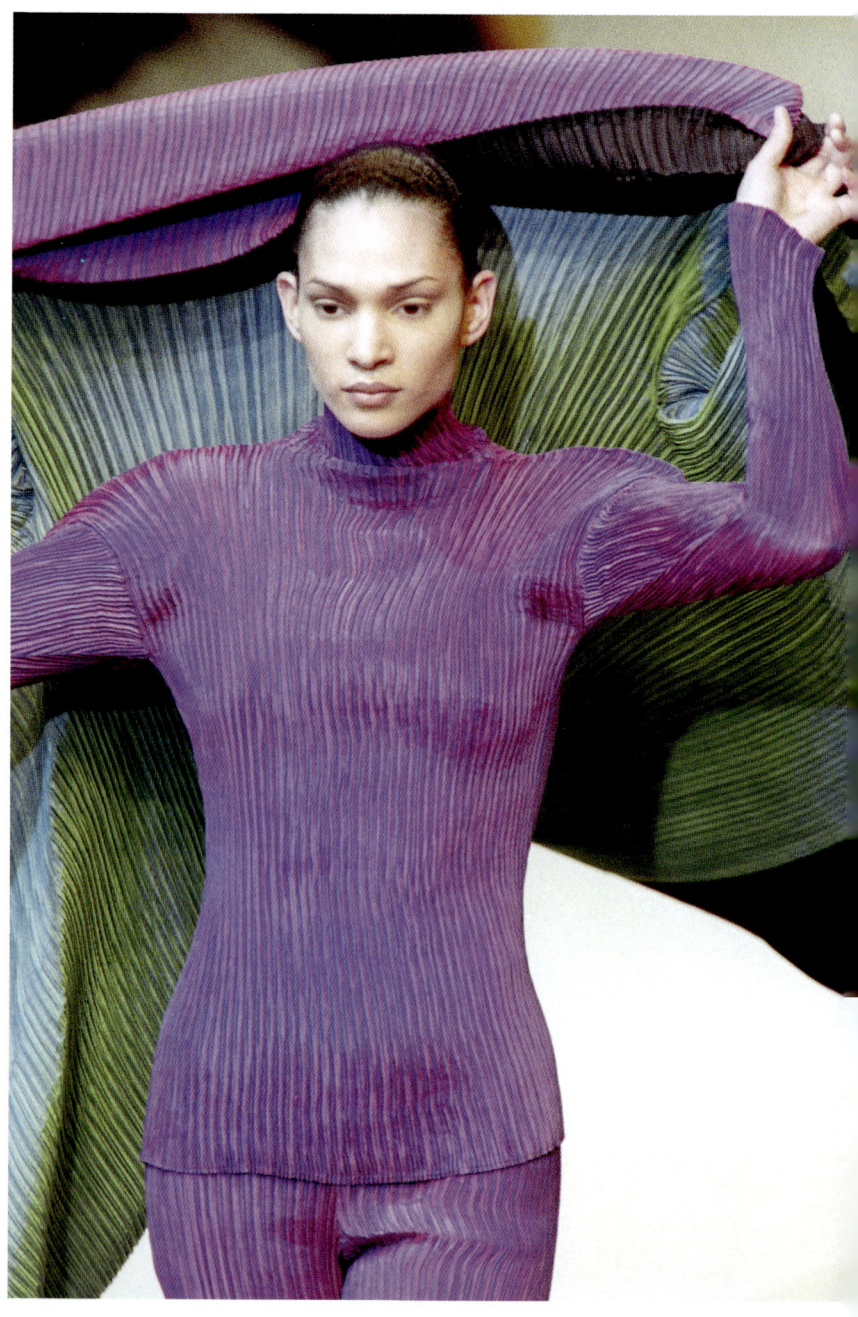

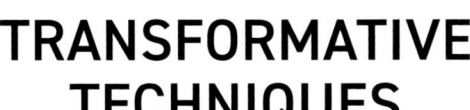

TRANSFORMATIVE TECHNIQUES

Miyake remained steadfast in his goal of making clothes that were worn by everyday people. While the designer's runway shows in Paris were spectacular, it was his innovation in pleated clothing that brought him closer to his ideal customer.

Using polyester material that had not been pleated before sewing (the regular way of working), Miyake manufactured these pieces at least three times larger than the final garment's size, and then cut and sewed the fabrics before compressing them using pressure and steam heat. The result was pleats that held their shape permanently and could be machine-washed and folded flat or stored in a suitcase but still look pristine when unpacked.

OPPOSITE A model wears a Pleats Please reversible cape and trousers with matching top from A/W 1995.

For Miyake, pleats were the result of his search for functional garments as well as his fascination with material surfaces. While he had experimented with stretchy fabrics via his tattoo collection from the 70s, those body stockings had limited appeal. So in his approach to developing pleats, he used polyester, a light and inexpensive fabric, blended with tricot jersey to give it some stretch.

RIGHT AND OPPOSITE From S/S 2001.

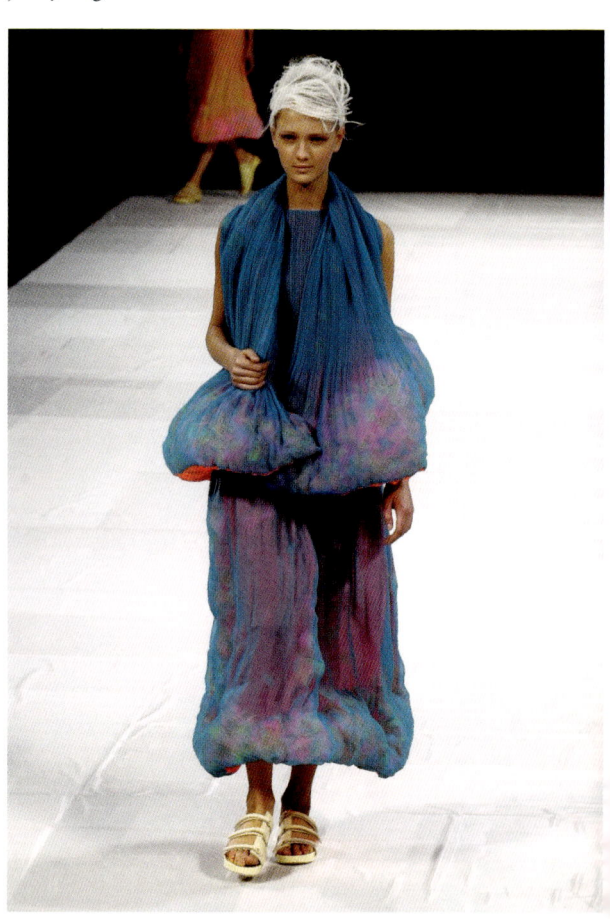

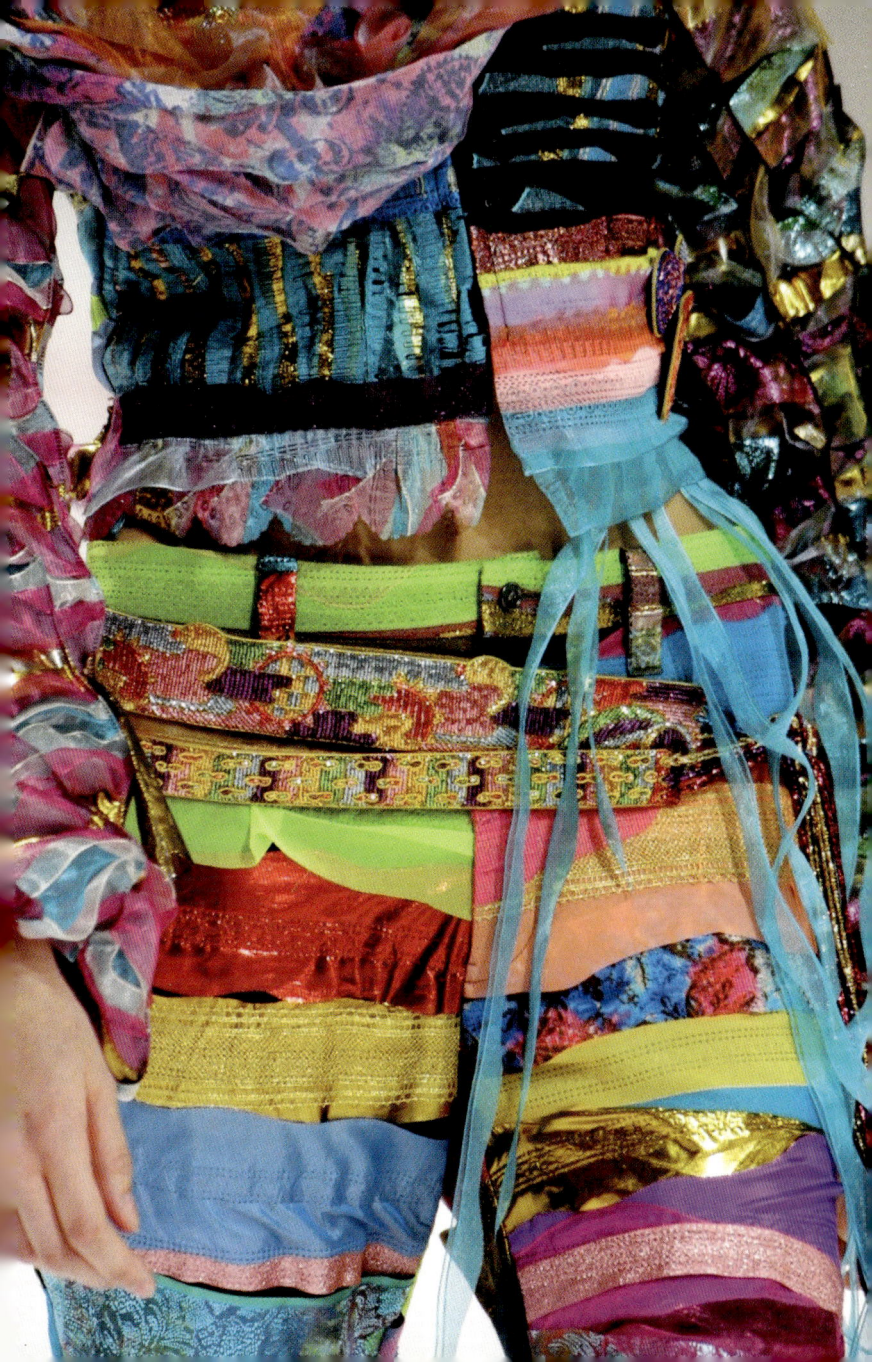

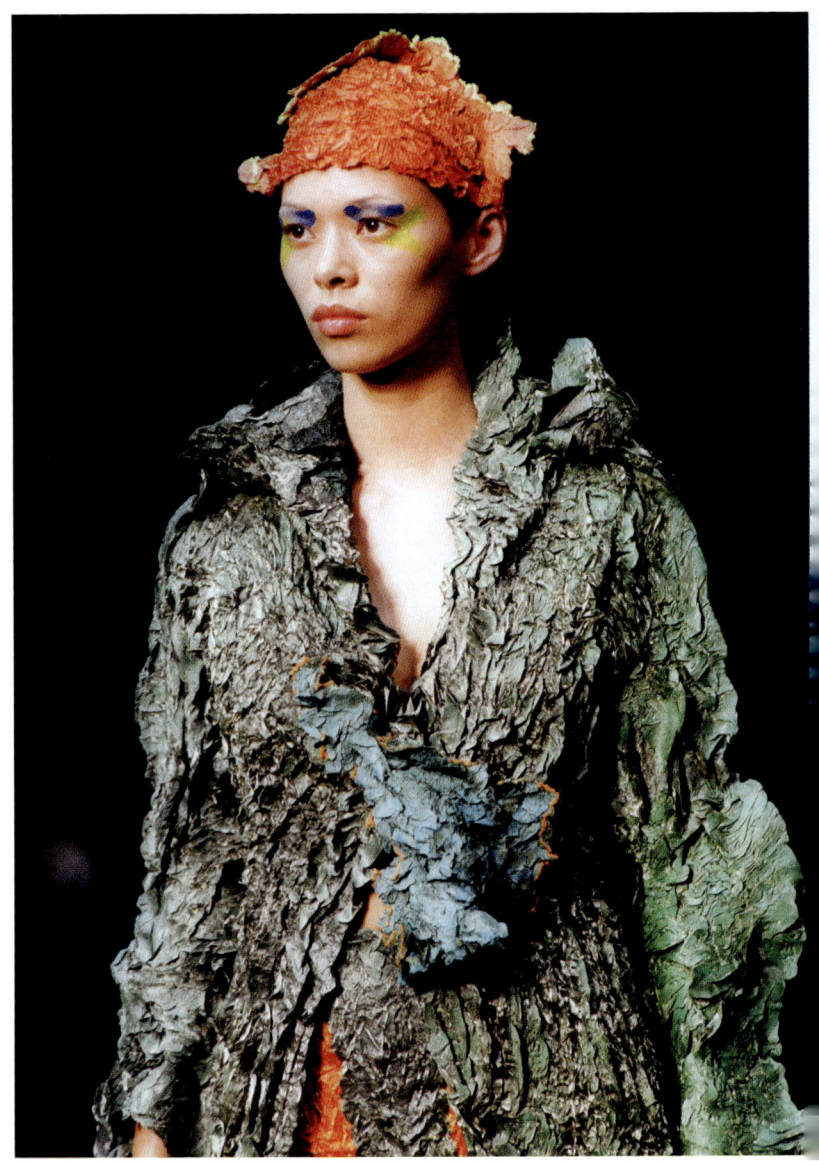

The pleated clothes served as an alternative to jeans, the archetype of Western democratic clothing, but were more visually pleasing. "If you take T-shirts or pairs of jeans, they can never cause any sort of surprise since people always know what to expect from them," said Miyake in the exhibition catalogue, *Making Things*. "I prefer to surprise people, to cause emotion. I would also like those who wear my clothes to feel free to adapt them and recreate them in their own way."

The accordion-like designs were first introduced as part of Issey Miyake's main line in 1988 and became a standalone brand, Pleats Please, in 1993 – the year Miyake patented his method. Inspiration came, in part, from Japanese origami. The other source of inspiration was the work of Spanish couturier

BELOW AND OPPOSITE From A/W 2000.

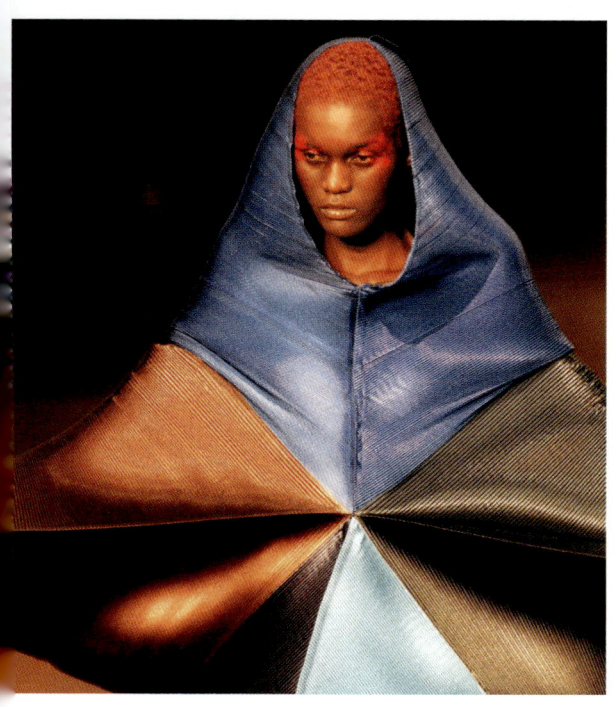

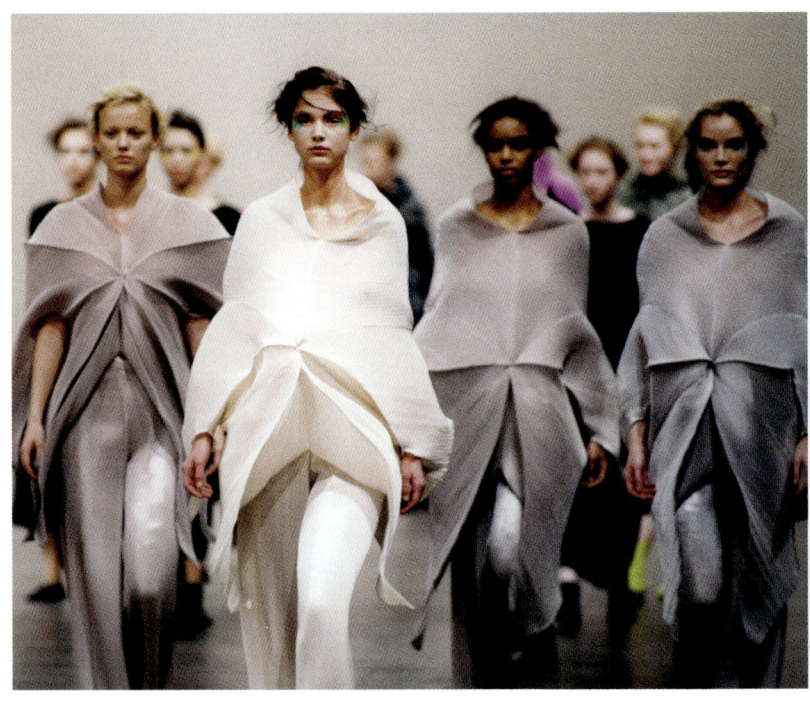

Mariano Fortuny, who revived a Grecian pleating system and perfected this in his one-size-fits-all Delphos garments, first created around 1907.

The idea had been percolating in Miyake's mind since the "A-Un" exhibit, as he explained in the book *Pleats Please Issey Miyake*, published by Taschen in 2012: "After the exhibition I became convinced that I had already accomplished everything that I could. And so I began to think about a new journey upon which to embark."

Miyake's technique transformed the appearance of the otherwise ordinary material and also created clothing that was comfortable and easy to care for, challenging traditional

notions that high fashion was high maintenance and making it
ideal for the modern age. Each year, the brand has continued to
add new colours, patterns and shapes to its pleats collection –
now Miyake's most recognizable invention.

Among Miyake's other groundbreaking designs was A-POC
("A Piece of Cloth"), created in collaboration with Dai Fujiwara
in 1998. Fujiwara had been tinkering with an abandoned
knitting machine that he had discovered and experimented
with the old technology to see if he could produce new fabrics.
Miyake encouraged this pursuit.

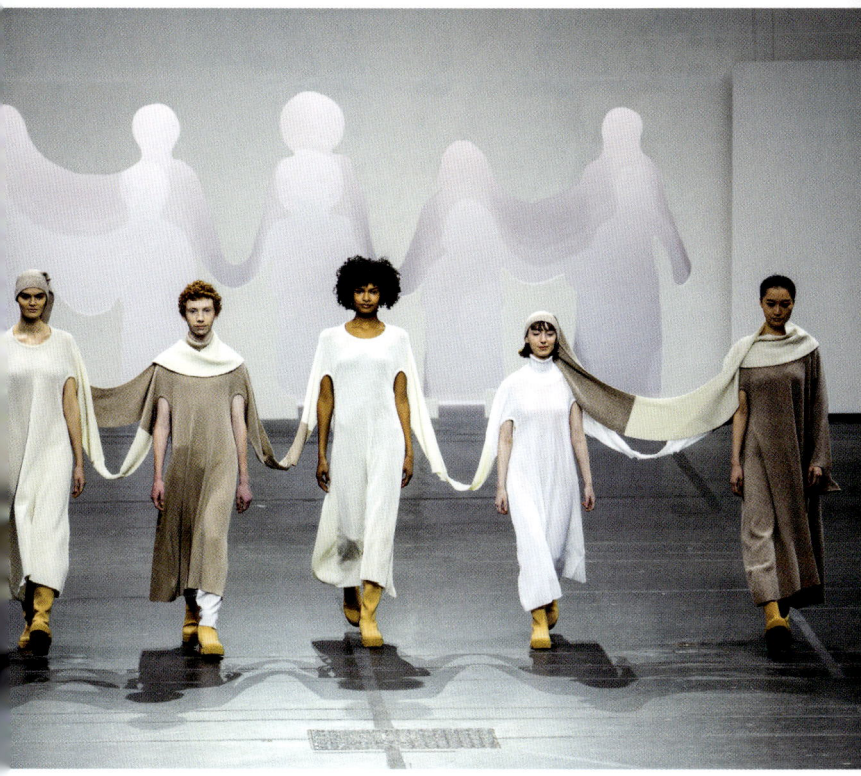

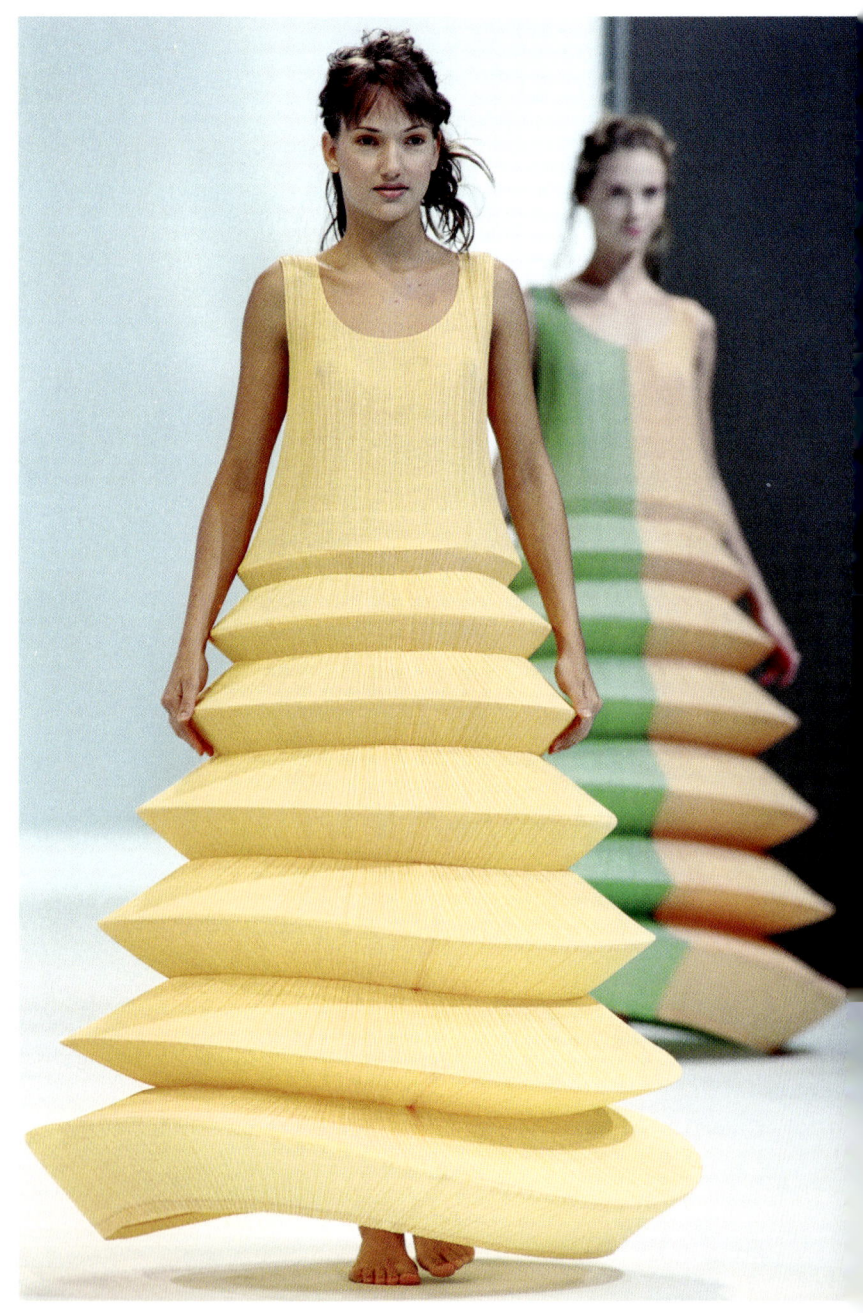

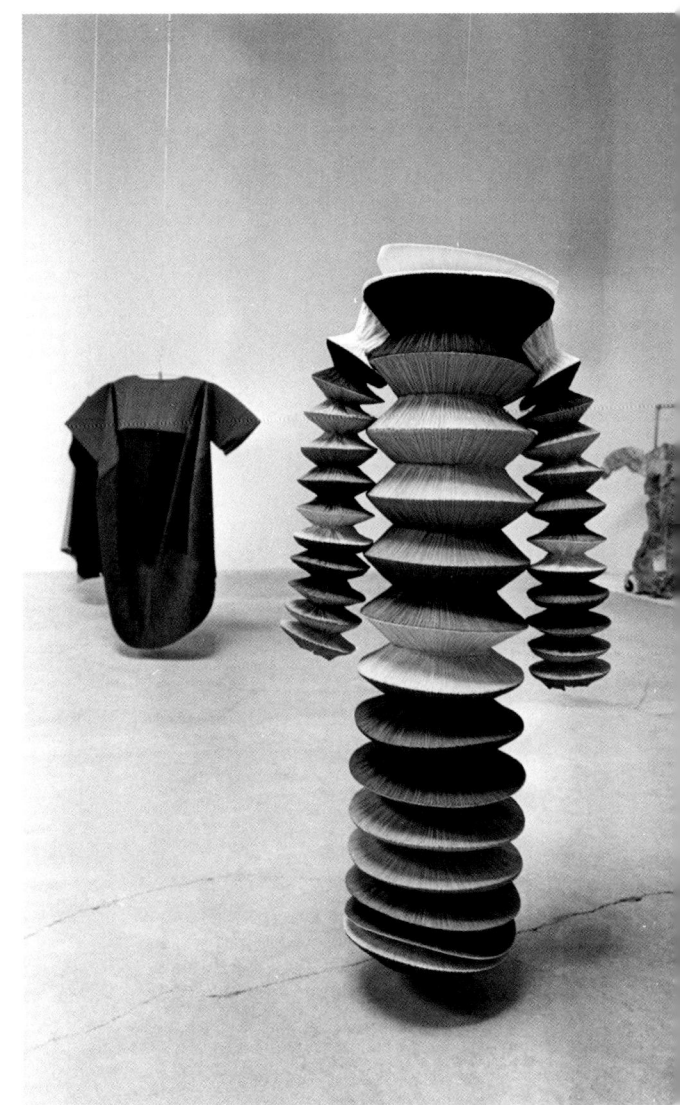

OPPOSITE Models wear Pleats Please dresses with wired hoops as part of the show for S/S 1995.

RIGHT Issey Miyake's designs on display at the "Making Things" exhibition presented by Ace Gallery, New York, 1999–2000.

The result was a single thread fed into a computer-driven weaving machine that churned out a cylinder, about 1.5m (5ft) wide, like a giant tube sock. Garments were "finished" by the client, who could cut and customize its final length. Like the kimono, the main principle was not to cut into woven cloth but to respect the integrity of the material and to instead use its shape to dress the body.

"A-POC unleashes the freedom of imagination. It's for people who are curious, who have inner energy – the energy of life and living," Miyake told *Newsweek* in 2002.

RIGHT AND OPPOSITE Issey Miyake and Dai Fujiwara's A-POC Queen Textile, 1997.

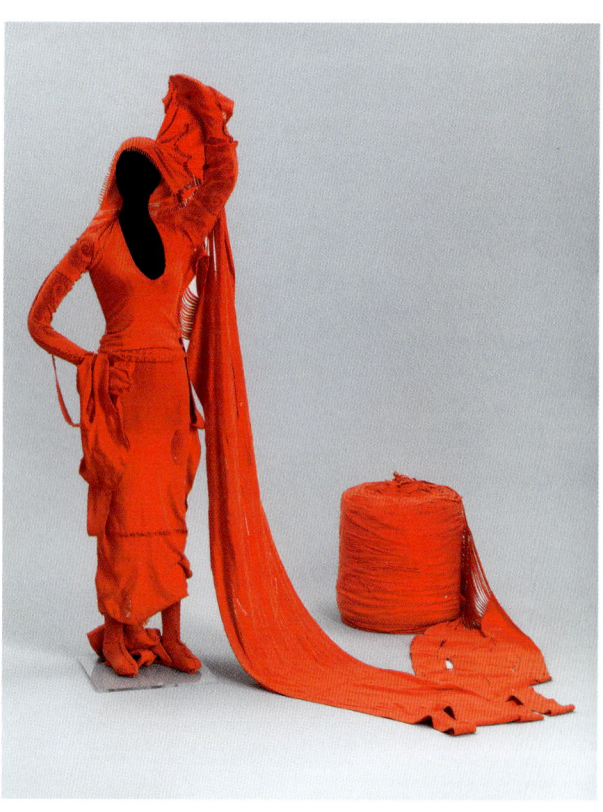

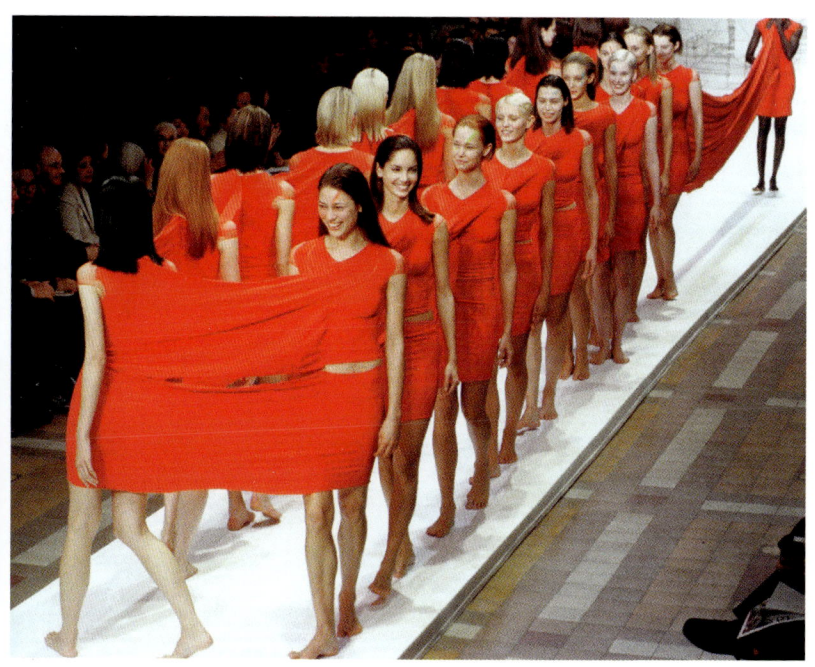

A-POC caught the eye of British-Israeli architect and artist Ron Arad, who collaborated with Miyake on a project called Gemini. Displayed at the 2006 Milan Furniture Fair, the body-hugging "outfit" was made of A-POC fabric – presented as a cover for Arad's stackable plastic Ripple Chair, it could also be worn by a person as a jacket.

"You attack the fabric with scissors and it doesn't fray. It's amazing. It's the sort of thing that could only come from Miyake and his collaborators," Arad told the *Financial Times* in 2014, describing A-POC as "the most exciting thing that has happened in industrial design." He continued: "The more sophisticated a machine gets, the less machine-like the product is. And that sums up A-POC for me."

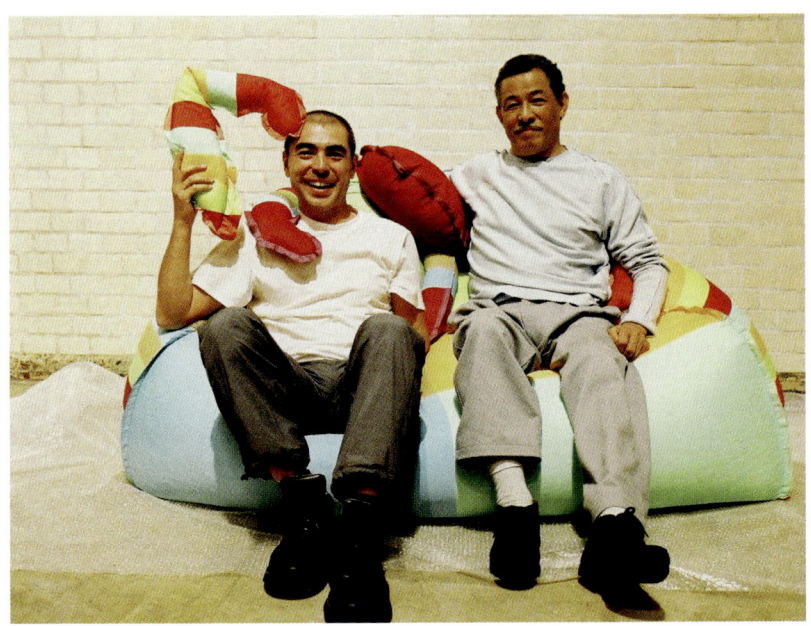

Miyake and Fujiwara hoped to push the A-POC process in directions that would revolutionize how mass-market goods such as upholstery and jeans were manufactured because no sewing was involved. The new approach was successful in Tokyo, but internationally it was slower to catch on – as Miyake and his team observed when the brand opened a dedicated A-POC Paris store in September 2000.

Conceptually it proved to be difficult for some Western fashion buyers to grasp. At the time, *Vogue*'s Anna Wintour remarked that Japanese designers' clothes were "too difficult to wear" to be a commercial success.

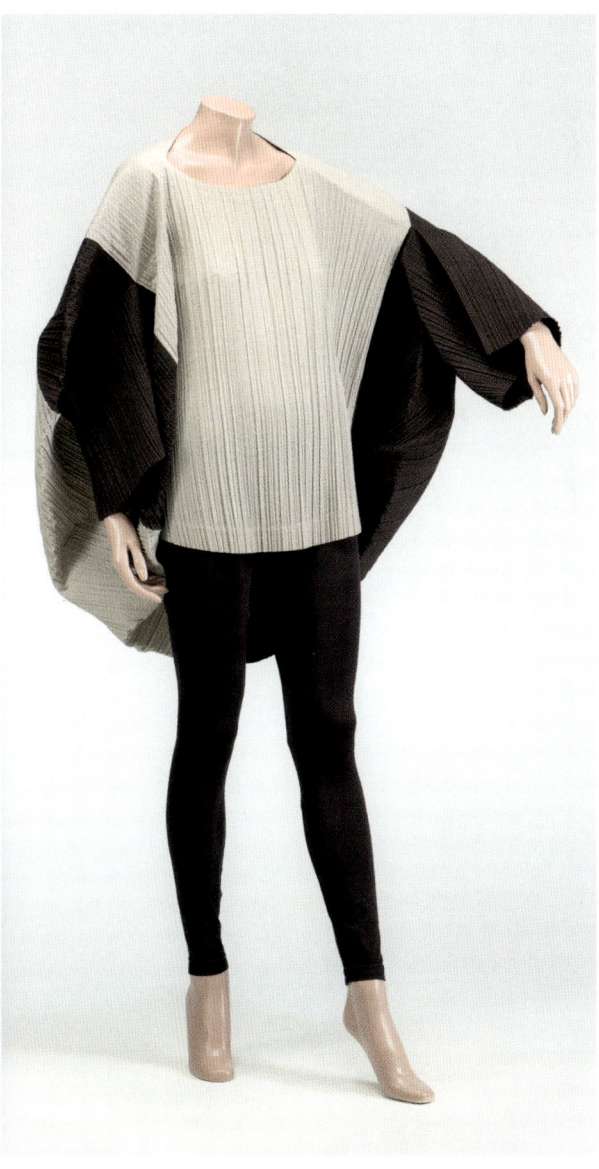

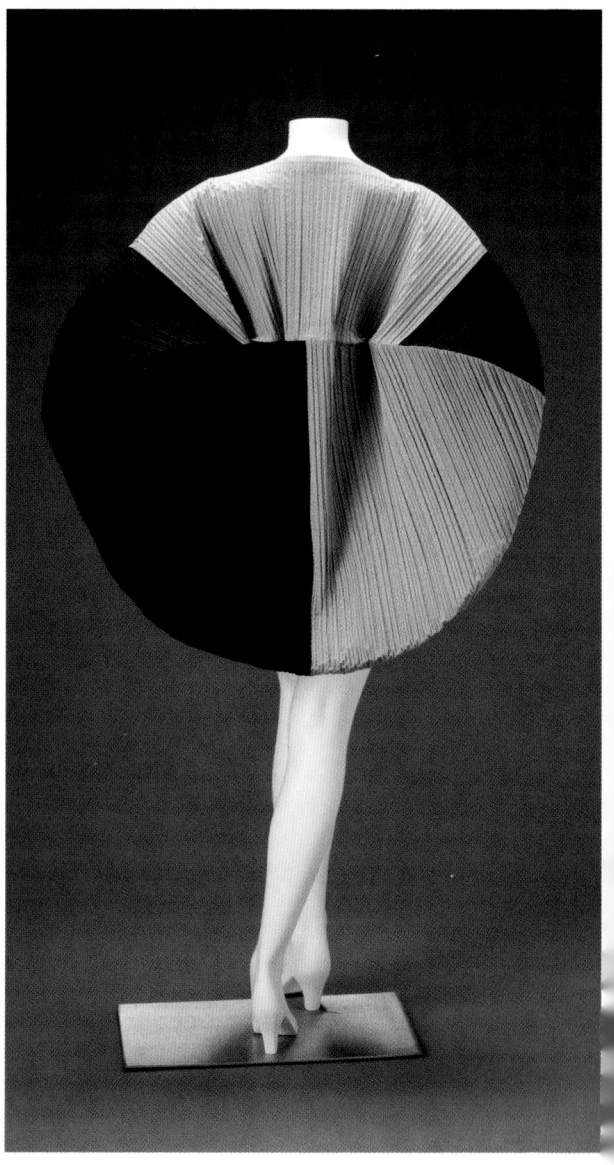

RIGHT From Issey Miyake's Rhythm Pleats series, 1990.

BELOW Issey Miyake's designs on display at the "Making Things" exhibition presented by Ace Gallery, New York, 1999–2000.

OVERLEAF Issey Miyake's designs on display at the "Making Things" exhibition, presented by the Fondation Cartier pour l'art contemporain, Paris, 1998.

Pieces from all of Miyake's unique and extraordinary lines are now included in the collections of museums worldwide, including the Victoria and Albert Museum in London, the Metropolitan Museum of Art and Museum of Modern Art in New York, and the Los Angeles County Museum of Art. And what makes them particularly noteworthy is that they were not only conceived as a beautiful solution to everyday needs, but they're also just as functional.

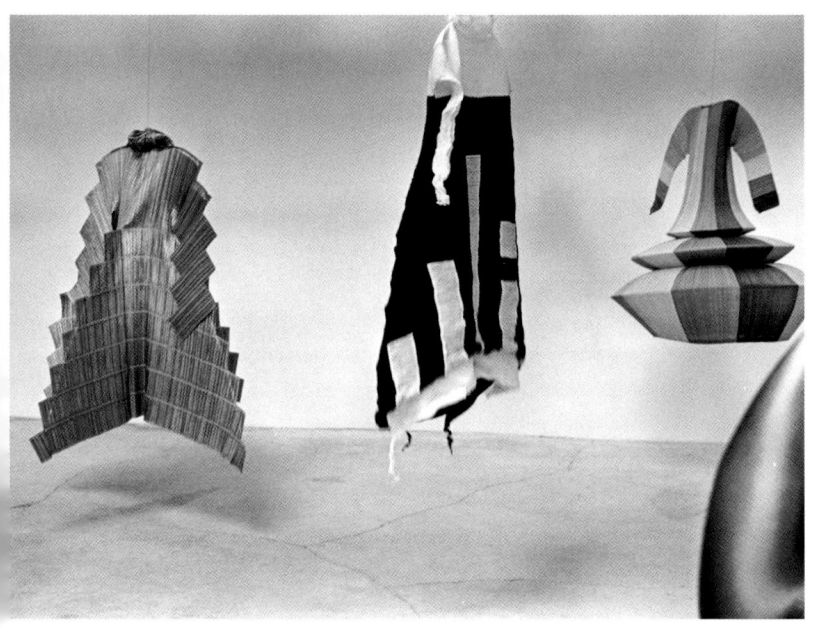

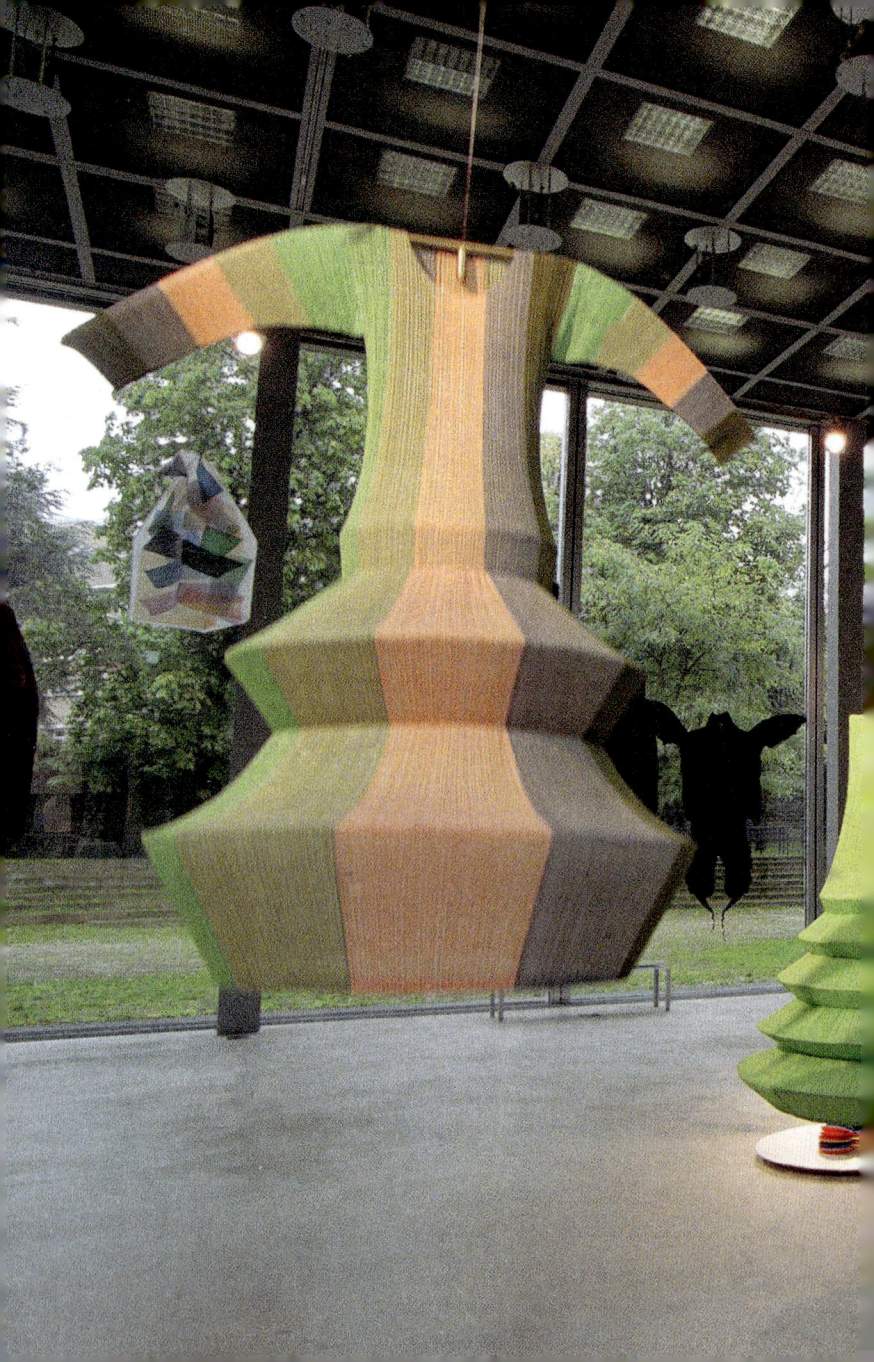

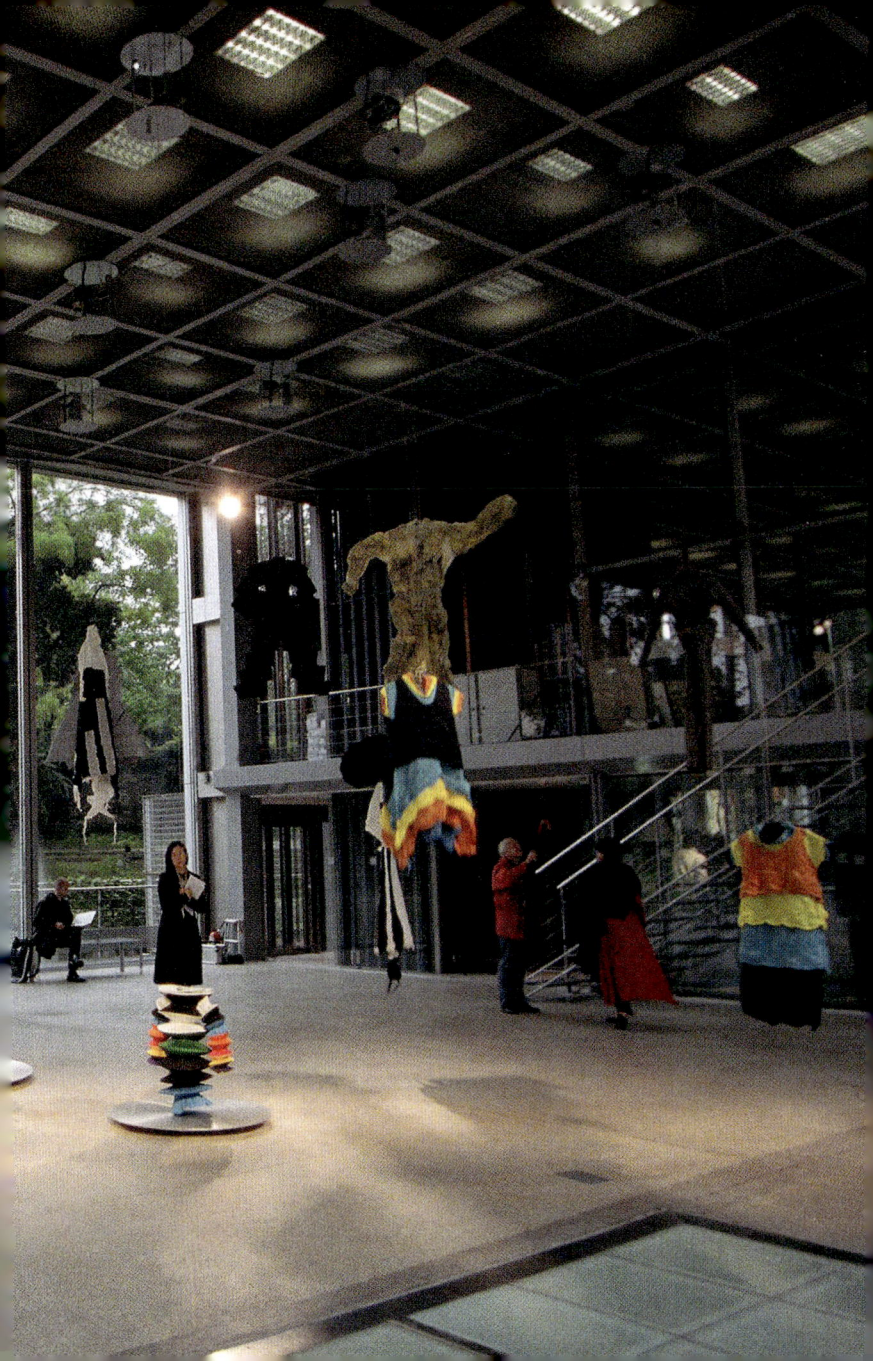

COLLABORATORS
AND MUSES

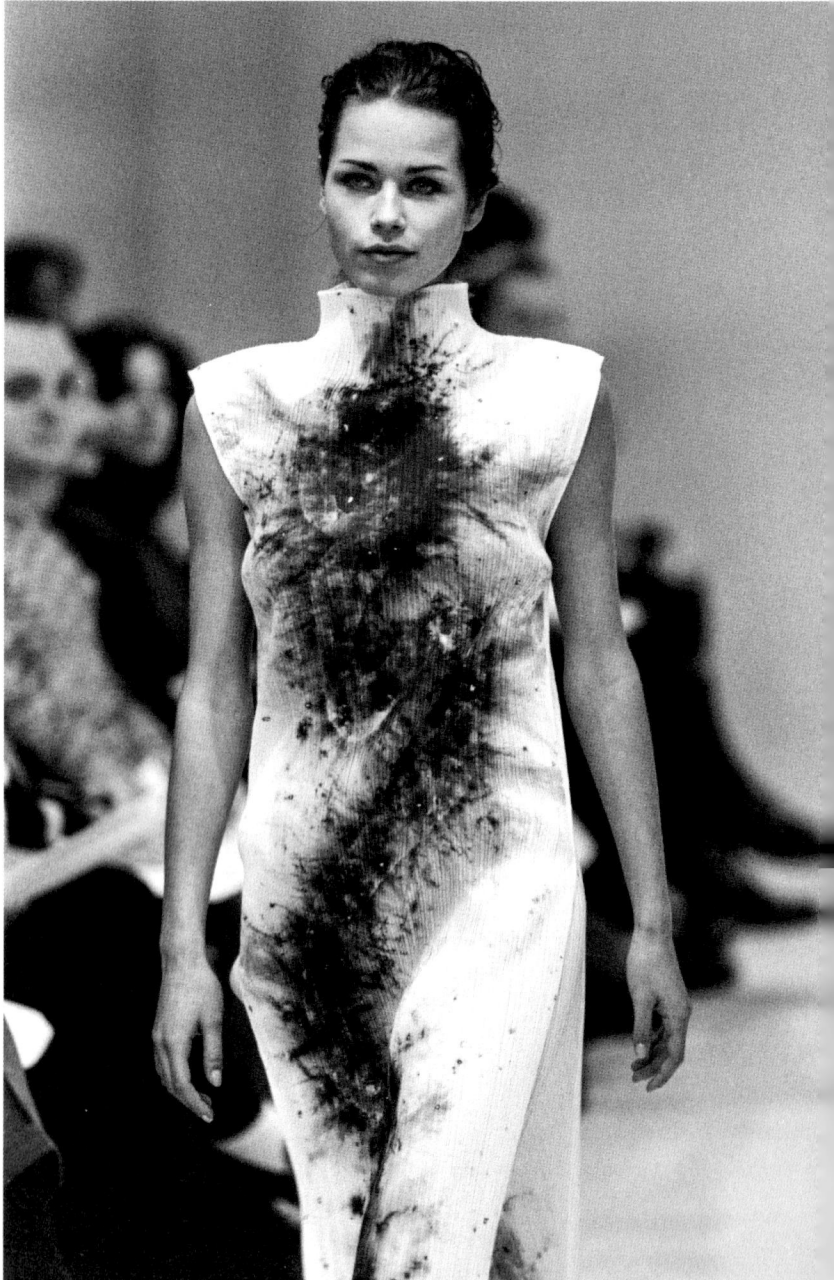

ISSEY'S INSPIRATION

Miyake, who never regarded himself as either an artist or a fashion designer, made the distinction between the two harder to discern. While Irving Penn was among the most notable of his collaborators, Miyake also embarked on memorable collaborations with other photographers as well as artists, dancers and architects.

As a young man impressed by Noguchi's ideals and creative vision, Miyake sought out drawings, photographs and any other output he could find by the architect. When Miyake set off for Paris in the 1960s, a photograph of Noguchi's work was one of the few items he took with him. The pair finally met in the mid 1970s, a turning point at which the hero of Miyake's youth became a friend and mentor.

Throughout their careers, Miyake and Noguchi were preoccupied with simplicity and form and favoured direct expression. Miyake has frequently credited Noguchi for all that he knows about space and proportion. The two artists partnered on the exhibition "Isamu Noguchi and Issey Miyake: Arizona"

OPPOSITE Issey Miyake's collaboration with artist Cai Guo-Qiang.

in June 1997. Staged at the Museum of Contemporary Art in Kagawa, it was inspired by the interaction of American and Japanese cultures. Today, one of Noguchi's final sculptures sits in the courtyard of the Miyake Design Studio in Tokyo.

OPPOSITE From S/S 1995

OVERLEAF From A/W 1998.

Miyake also gave back by opening the doors for young creatives. In 1974, he commissioned Shiro Kuramata, then an up-and-coming talent, to design his first store in Tokyo. (Until his death in 1991, Kuramata continued to design dozens of retail spaces for Miyake, later covering some of them in his trademark terrazzo infused with coloured glass.)

Architect David Chipperfield also caught Miyake's eye early on and in 1985 he was hired to design Miyake's store in London. As Chipperfield wrote on his personal Instagram commemorating Miyake in 2022, "Designing his shop on Sloane Street marked the beginning of my career. For three years afterwards, I travelled around Japan designing a series of little shops for him. It was a fundamental, formative part of my design experience."

In 1990, Miyake designed dance costumes for *The Loss of Small Detail*, a ballet created by the American choreographer William Forsythe, then based in Frankfurt. While ultralight polyester jersey material was already part of many designers' clothing vocabulary, it was used in a new and challenging way by Miyake. After studying the dancers' movements, he created 200 to 300 different garments for the dancers to wear in each performance. This later inspired him to use dancers rather than models on his runways in Paris.

Another monumental project for Miyake was the Olympic uniform he designed in 1992 for Lithuania, which was participating in the Games for the first time in 64 years, having gained independence from the Soviet Union. The challenge was designing for athletes of many different body sizes. Miyake turned to the technology he used for his pleated clothing

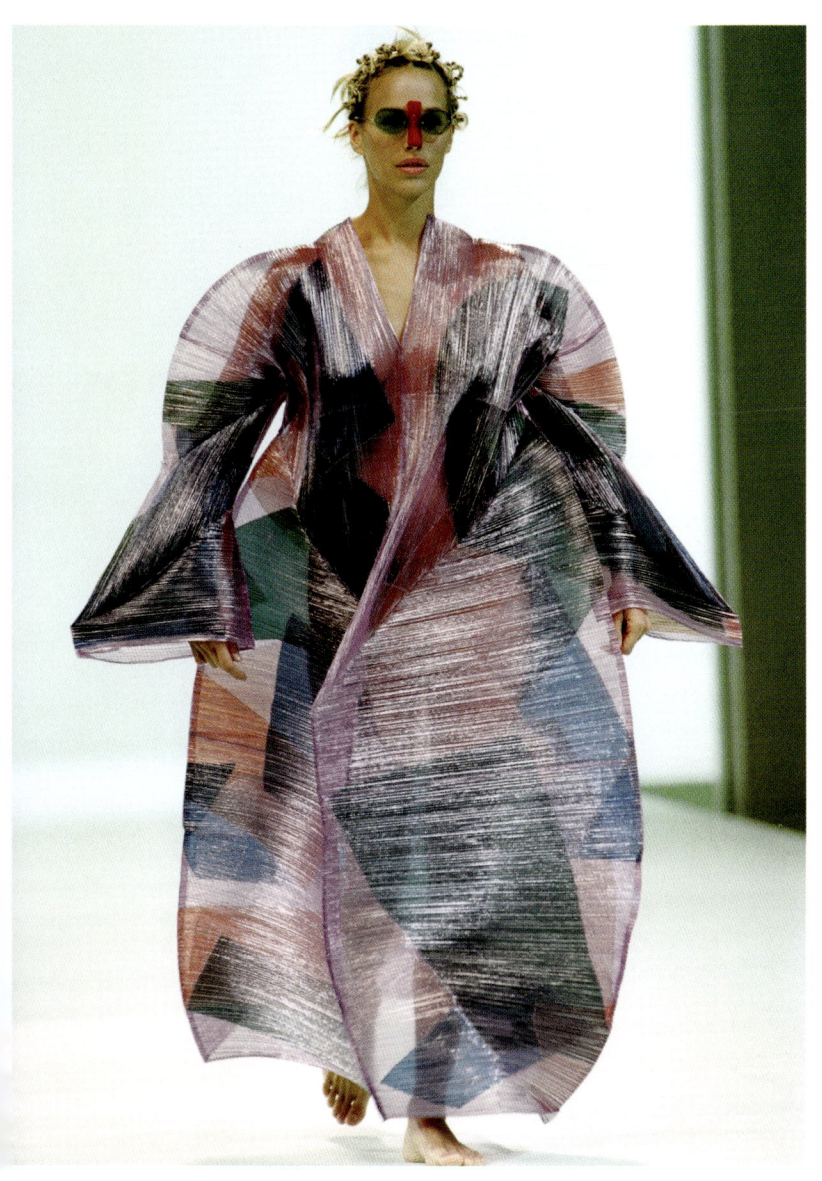

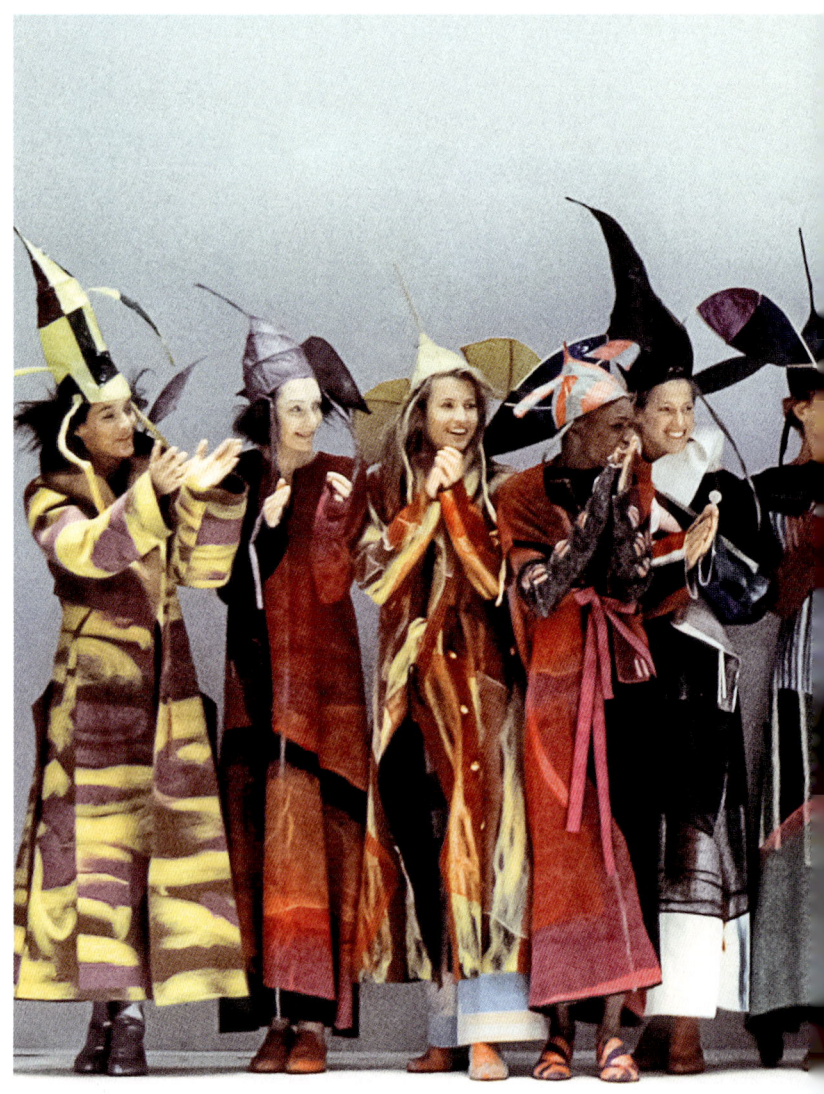

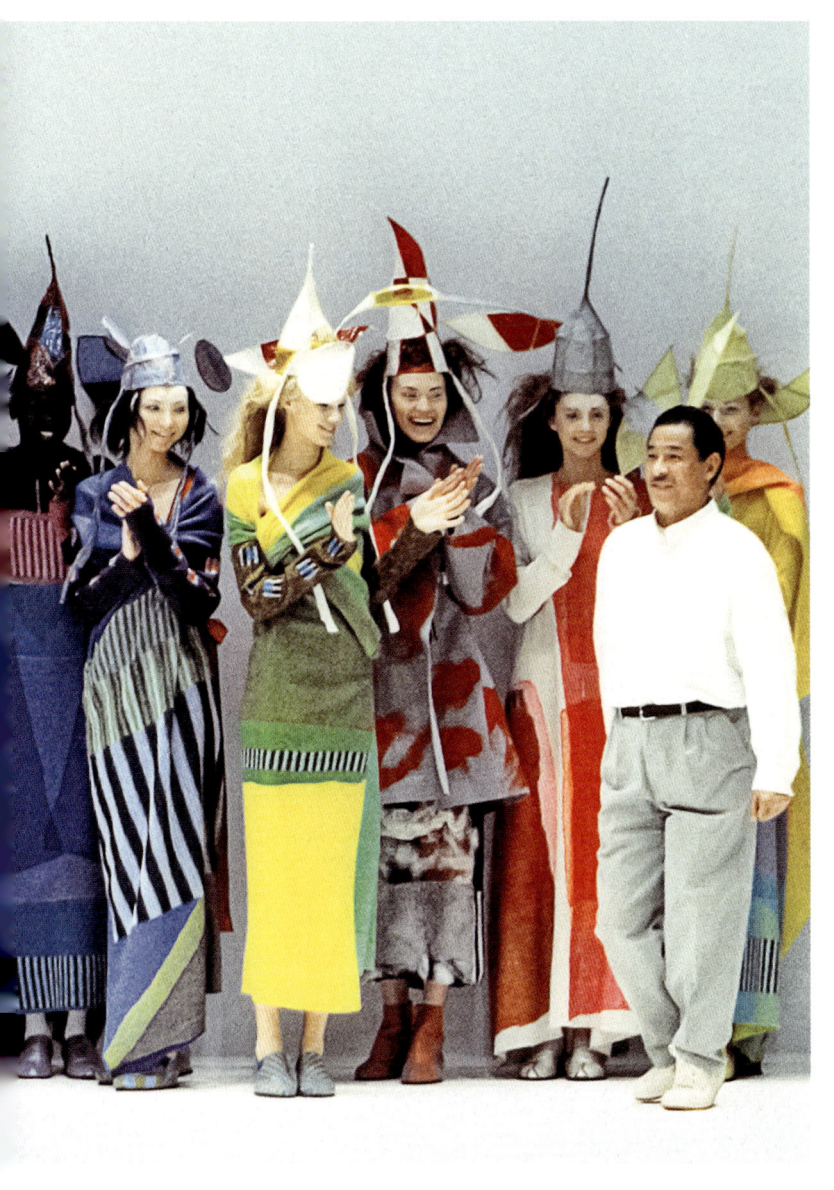

BELOW The 1992
Lithuanian Olympic
uniform, designed
by Issey Miyake, on
display at Tokyo's
National Art Center.

in order to create inclusive uniforms, which included a hooded jacket and trousers made from pleats, as well as a cap and shoes.

The fabric was provided by Toray Industries, the production was done by Mizuno Corporation and the pleating by Polytex Industry Co. The jacket collar featured the national flag and turned into a hood when fastened. A patchwork pattern of the Olympic logo, flag and country

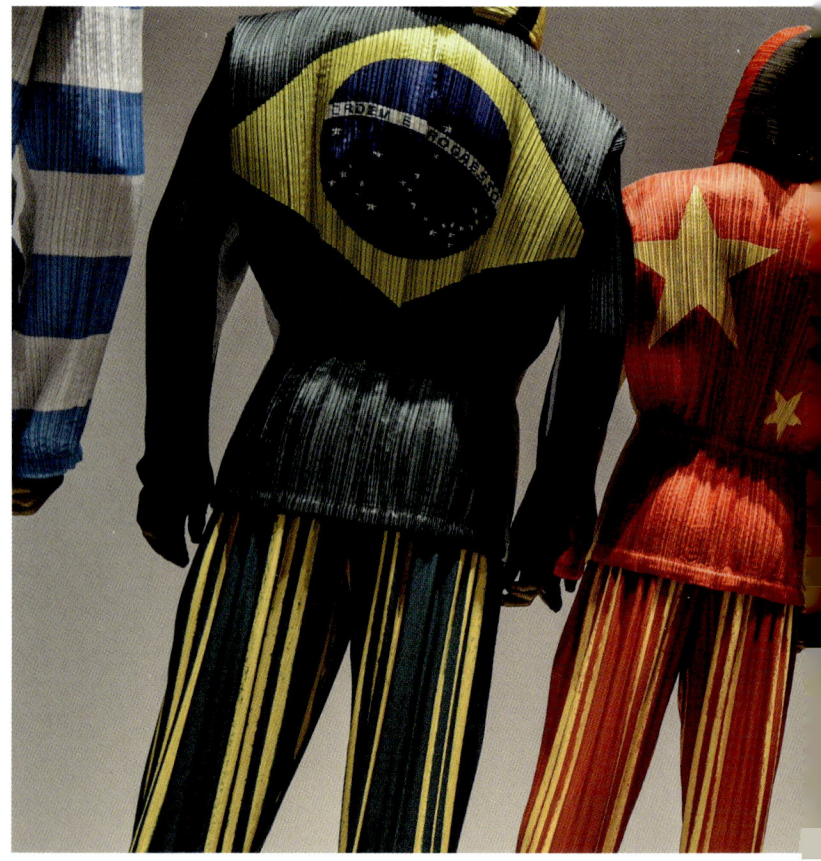

name was created several times larger than the final design to account for the contraction during pleating.

Until around 1996, Miyake's designs were largely neutral coloured, but he introduced more vivid colours and prints after his Guest Artist Series. From 1996 to 1998 he used his famous pleats as a canvas for collaboration with contemporary artists such as Yasumasa Morimura (1996), Nobuyoshi Araki (1997), Tim Hawkinson (1998) and Cai Guo-Qiang (1998).

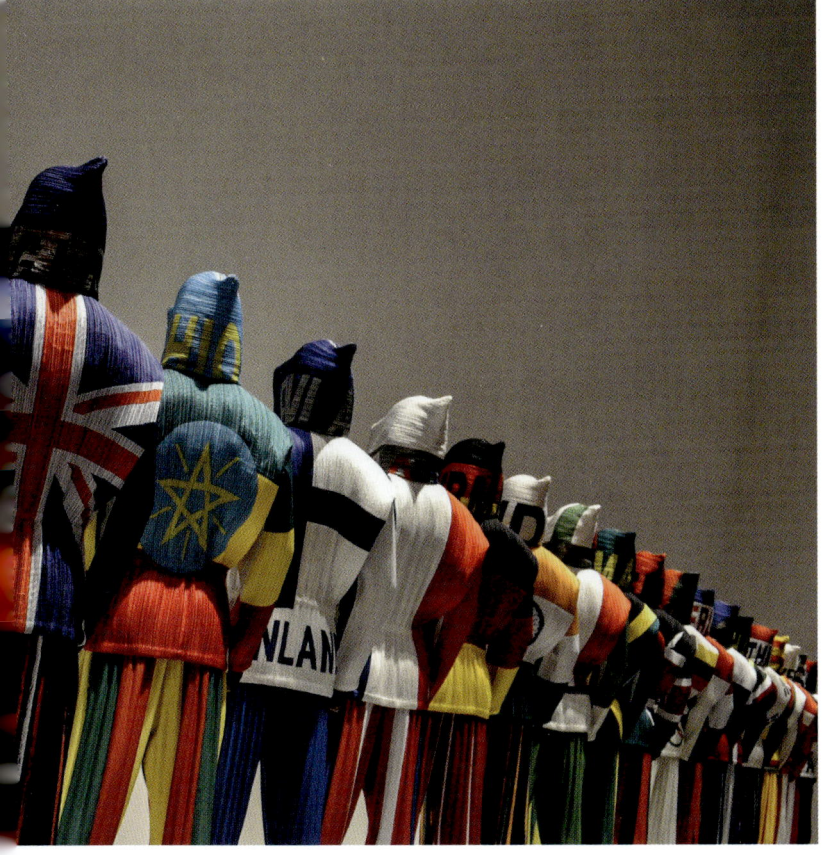

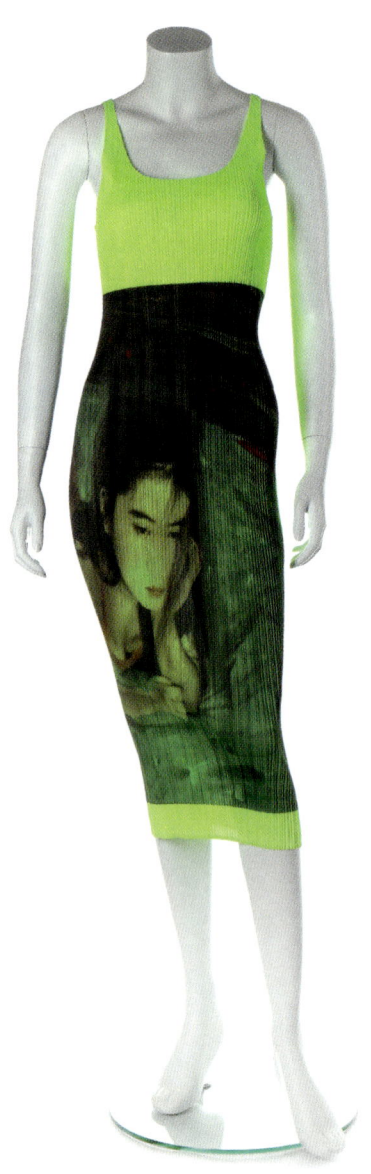

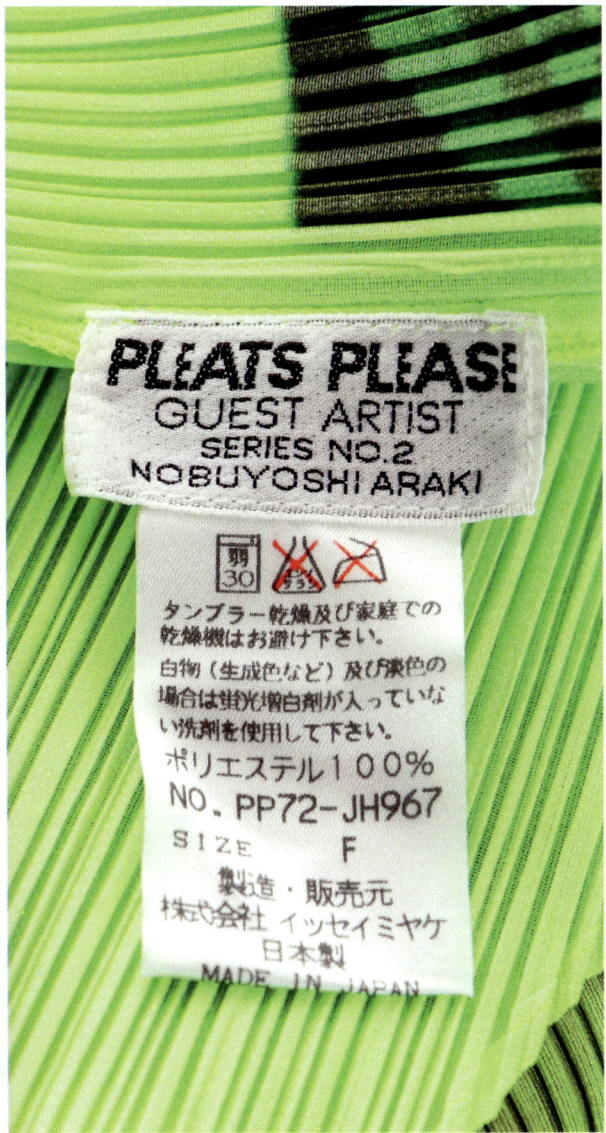

LEFT AND OPPOSITE The Pleats Please "Guest Artist Series" with Nobuyoshi Araki, 1997.

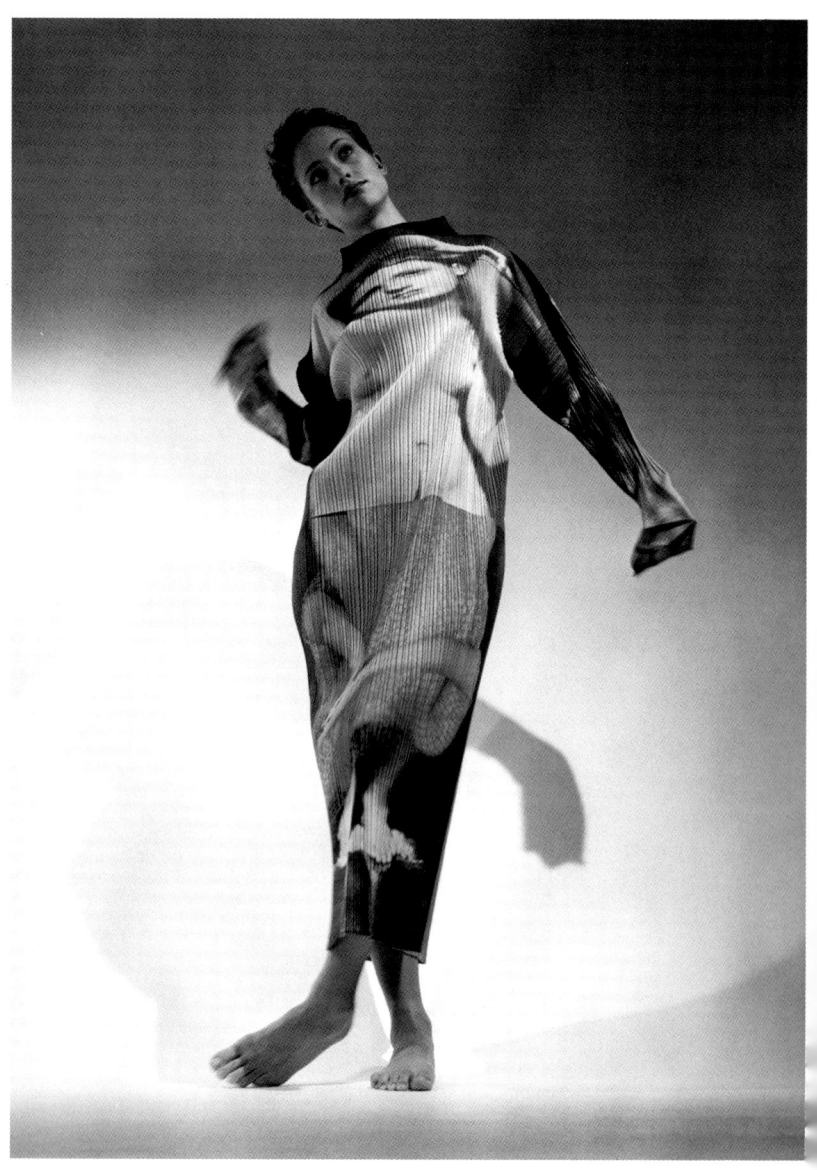

"I knew that I wanted to do something strange, something complex," he told the *ParisVoice* newspaper in 1998. "I did not want to choose an artist who was too fashionable but rather an individual who draws on provocative ideas. Perhaps also an artist who focuses on the body and eroticism."

Morimura, for example, uses his body as a vehicle for expression. When Miyake invited the artist to print a selection of his images onto a series of garments, Morimura chose pictures from the late 1980s that were inspired by *The Source*, an oil painting by French neoclassical painter Jean-Auguste-Dominique Ingres which took 36 years to complete. Keeping the top half of the naked model in the painting, Morimura added a photograph of his own body to the lower half. The result is a printed image that moves – and in that sense lives – according to the body that is wearing it.

Araki takes an autobiographical approach with his work and the pieces he created for Miyake are based on the theme of memory. Printed on the fabric before it is pleated, or in some cases afterwards, the photographs reveal or erase the image of a young woman or the artist's self-portrait, depending on the forms and movements of the wearer, much like Morimura's.

Self-portraits were also the focus of Hawkinson, whose body, stretched out in a bathtub, was the basis of a superimposed image that was then divided into thick sections and reproduced on graphic paper.

Meanwhile, Cai took inspiration from thousand-year-old Chinese traditions and incorporated fire in a performance, when Cai lit a trail of gunpowder that had been sprinkled over the garments, which had been placed on the ground in the form of a dragon, the Chinese symbol of life. Miyake transferred the resulting burn marks as prints on the clothing as part of the collaboration.

OPPOSITE The Pleats Please "Guest Artist Series" with Yasumasa Morimura, 1996.

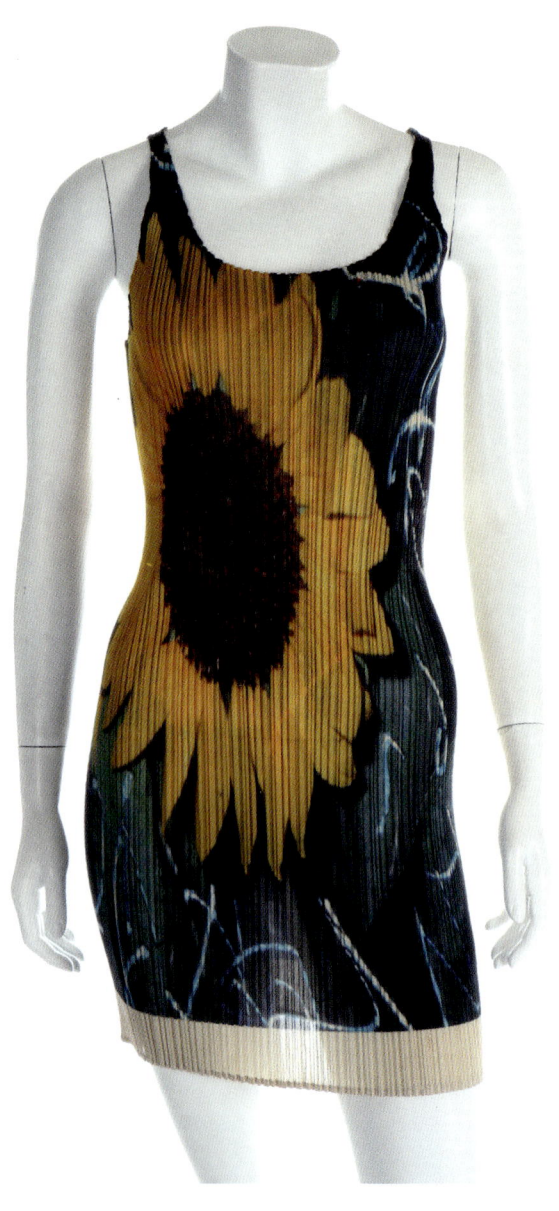

LEFT The Pleats
Please "Guest
Artist Series" with
Nobuyoshi Araki,
1997.

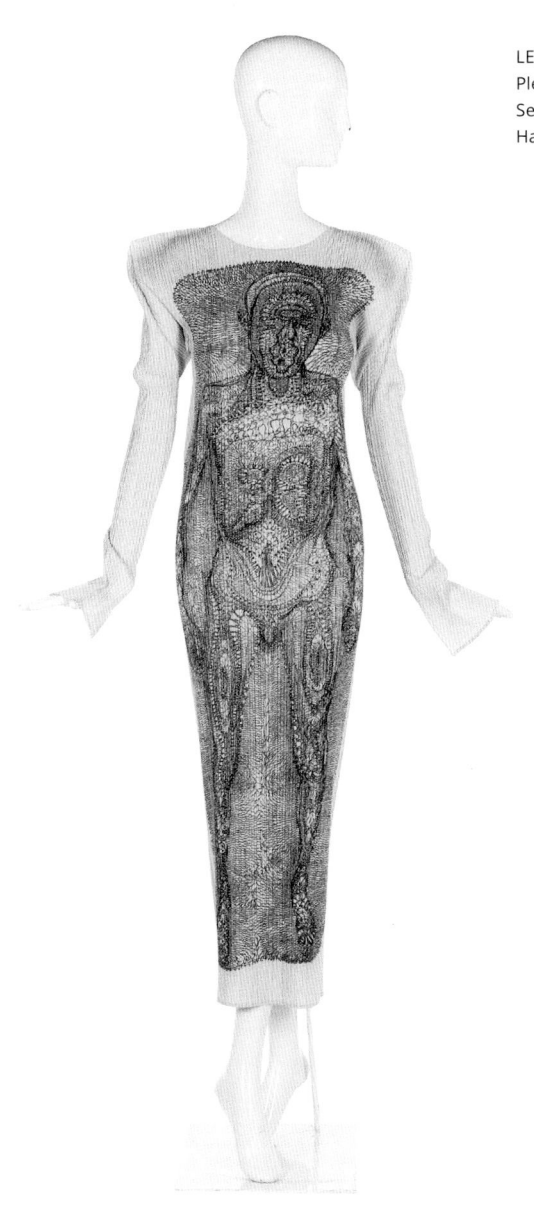

LEFT The Pleats Please "Guest Artist Series" with Tim Hawkinson, 1998.

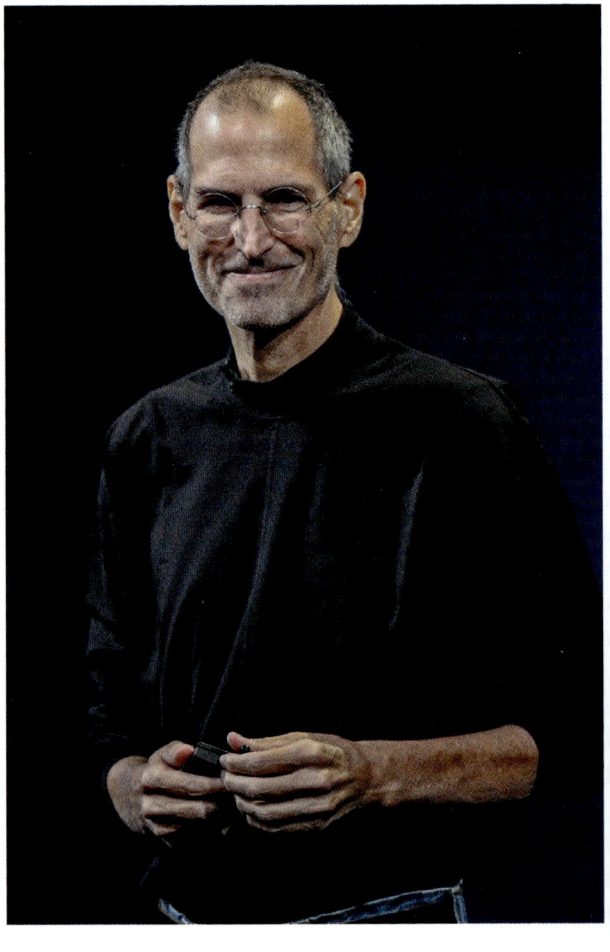

Miyake's influence exceeded the art world; one of his biggest
fans was Apple co-founder Steve Jobs, whose trademark black
turtleneck sweaters were designed by Miyake.

Author Walter Isaacson's biography of Jobs recounts the
American entrepreneur's gravitation towards Japanese culture

and its crafting principles. Jobs had wanted Miyake to create uniforms for all Apple employees. The idea came from a trip to Japan in the 1980s when the Apple co-founder visited Sony and saw the workers in the factories wearing matching uniforms.

Jobs asked then-chairman Akio Morita about it. "He looked very ashamed and told me that after the war, no one had any clothes, and companies like Sony had to give their workers something to wear each day," Jobs told his biographer, before his death, aged 56, in 2011.

Miyake had created a nylon jacket for Sony, that has removable sleeves and could be converted into a vest. Isaacson wrote that the uniform became part of Sony's signature style and "it became a way of bonding workers to the company." That appealed to Jobs, who then "called Issey and asked him to design a vest for Apple. I came back with some samples and told everyone it would be great if we would all wear these vests." However, his staff weren't keen on the idea and it never came to fruition. "Oh man, did I get booed off the stage," said Jobs.

Instead, Jobs decided on a signature outfit for himself. "I asked Issey to make me some of his black turtlenecks that I liked, and he made me 100 of them," he said. "I have enough to last for the rest of my life."

Miyake's black turtleneck was also adopted by another tech innovator, Elizabeth Holmes, who was later convicted of fraud in connection to her blood-testing company, Theranos. She had discovered Miyake through a former staffer, chief design architect Ana Arriola.

"She was very curious about Steve's attire and I explained to her that he was inspired by Sony's heritage of having Issey Miyake create a lot of the [Sony] line manager apparel," Arriola told podcast The Dropout. "I think she went off and tracked down who Issey Miyake was, and the rest is couture history."

PLEATS,
MENSWEAR AND
FRAGRANCE

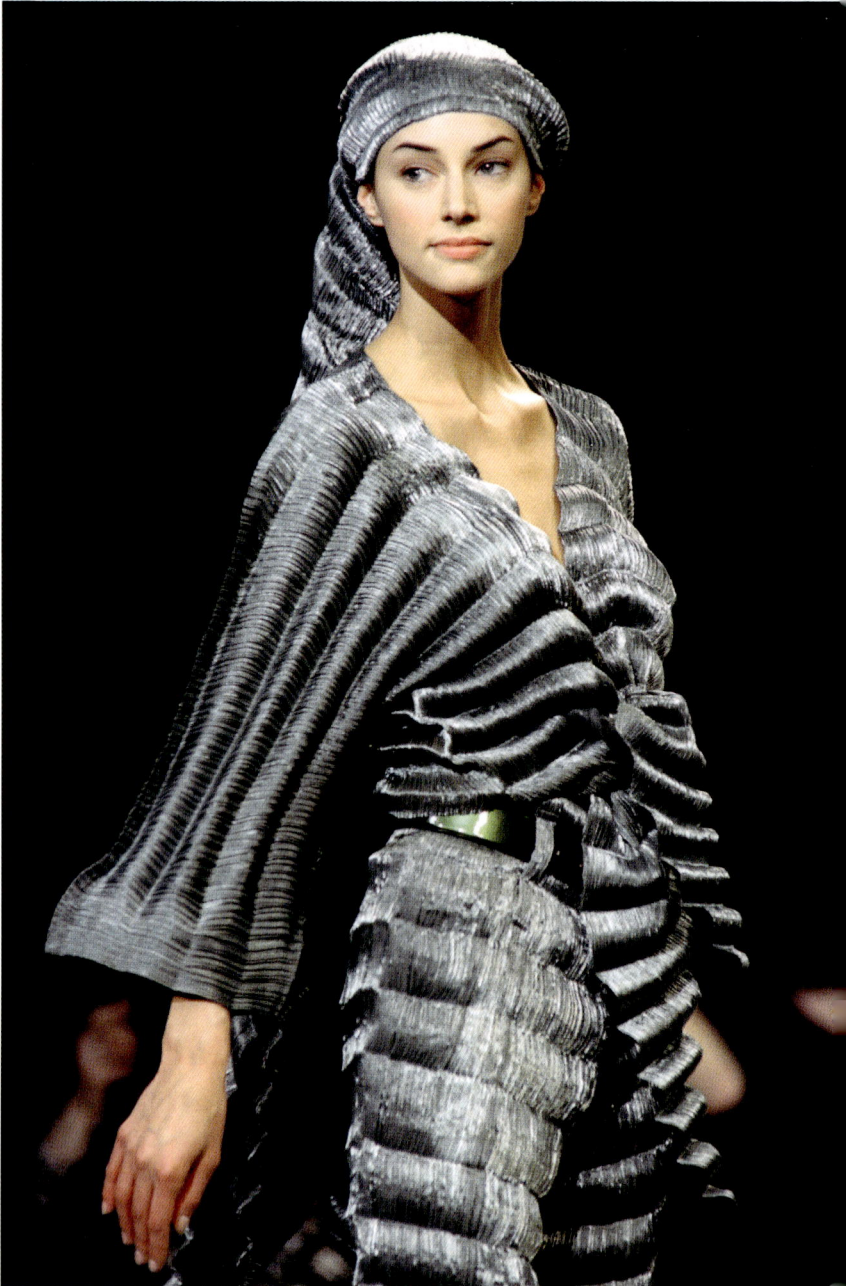

CONSTRUCTIBLE FASHION

In 2013, two decades after Pleats Please, Miyake introduced a new brand for men, Homme Plissé. Using his innovative garment pleating techniques, this offered wrinkle-resistant casualwear as an alternative to everyday clothing. Developed with the male customer in mind, the pleats do not cling to the body, making it easy to move about, and are easy to maintain and carry around when travelling. Compared to the Pleats Please range, Homme Plissé also came in looser variations, at times with graphic patterns and edgier treatments.

Wearing Homme Plissé, it's easy for the wearer to forget about their body. They may even forget about the garment itself. Instead, they are likely to feel comfort and space, making it little wonder that Homme Plissé has been adopted not only by designers and architects but also by gymnasts, acrobats and dancers, many of whom often feature in complex choreography staged as part of the brand's seasonal presentations.

OPPOSITE From A/W 1994.

For Homme Plissé's Autumn/Winter 2014 collection, Miyake took inspiration from capoeira, a Brazilian martial art historically disguised as a dance and performed to musical instruments and traditional songs. Miyake's intention was to demonstrate his clothing's ability to withstand vigorous activity. The movements of capoeira and its rhythmic music have been linked to the origins of the samba. It is also said to have influenced breakdancing.

Movement continued to be the focus of Homme Plissé's shows in the years that followed. The Spring/Summer 2020 collection, for example, was shown in Place des Vosges, the oldest planned square in Paris. Choreographed by artistic director and performer Daniel Ezralow, it featured models meandering around the square's fountain, wearing pleated clothing in punchy, saturated colours, such as yellow, pink and blue. Some carried knapsacks or other bags. As an Afro-Brazilian female percussion troupe joined the fray, the pace quickened and models spun around and danced. Some were now wearing more pattern-infused looks, such as a chequered shirts or trousers, and kimono-style jackets. The mood was joyful and lively, as was Miyake's intention, which was to brighten everyday life and inspire people to express their individuality in a creative and original way.

Homme Plissé designs were initially seen as casual weekend wear, but increasingly relaxed office dress codes have led them to be worn during the week by customers. The brand has since introduced more formal styles, such as high-waisted trousers, button-down shirts and simple zip-up jackets, all made from knife-edge pleated polyester. Echoing Miyake's approach across his other lines, Homme Plissé has also collaborated with artists, such as French designer Ronan Bouroullec, whose recognizable strokes and abstract drawing were crafted with a Japanese felt-tip brush and transformed onto clothing.

OPPOSITE Homme Plissé Issey Miyake, S/S 2020.

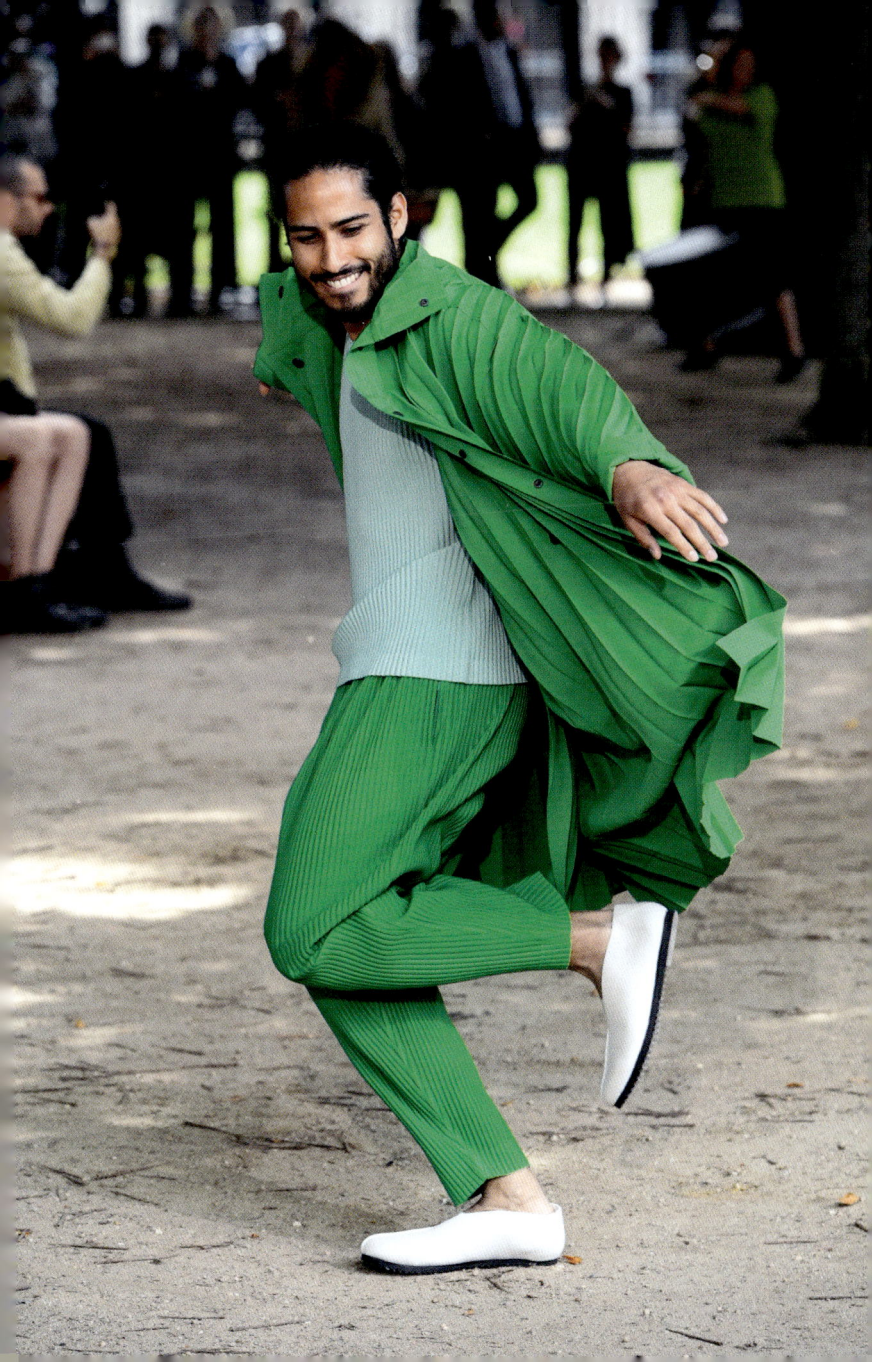

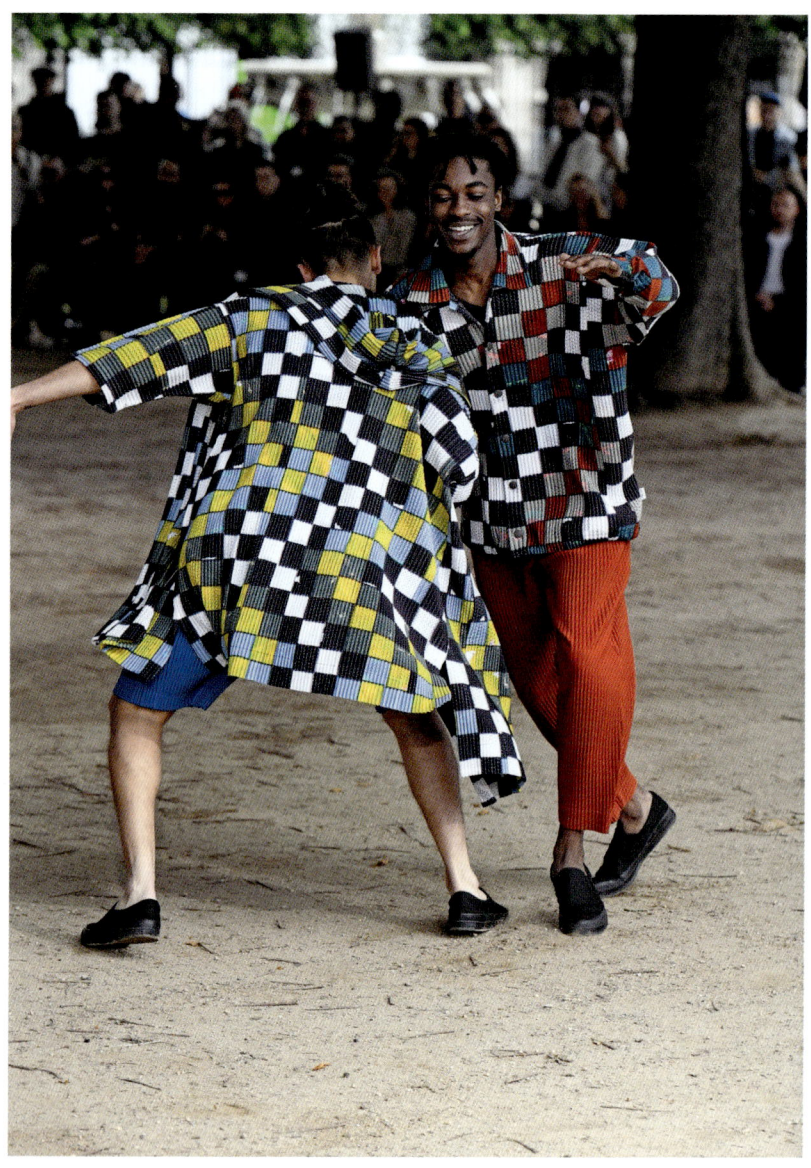

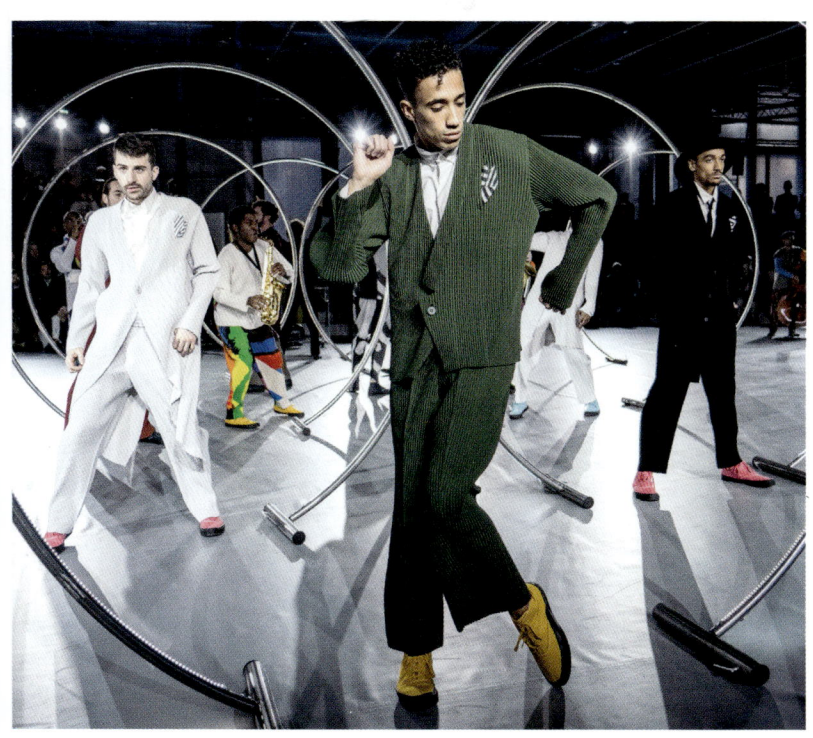

OPPOSITE Homme
Plissé Issey Miyake,
S/S 2020.

BELOW Issey
Miyake Menswear,
A/W 2021.

While the label is synonymous with an intellectual and uncluttered lifestyle, Miyake's clothes flatter all shapes and sizes – so much so that it has won over even the most enthusiastic luxury shoppers. When the curator Antwaun Sargent attended a Louis Vuitton menswear show in 2021, he told *GQ* magazine of his surprise to see how many men showed up in similar outfits. They were dressed, not in Louis Vuitton, but in shirts and trousers from Homme Plissé.

Among Homme Plissé's fans is Rafael de Cárdenas. The interior designer recently told *Town & Country* magazine that wearing Homme Plissé is "a good way to look smart when you're actually wearing sweatpants." De Cardenas is one of

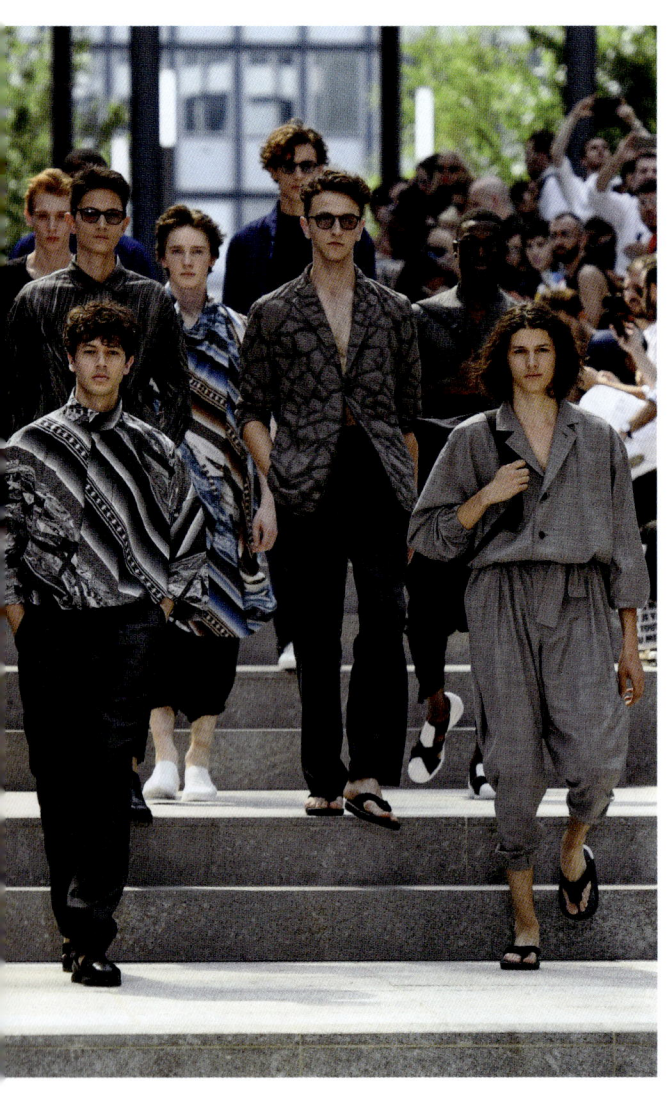

LEFT Issey Miyake
Menswear S/S
2018.

OPPOSITE Dancers
perform on the
runway for S/S
2018.

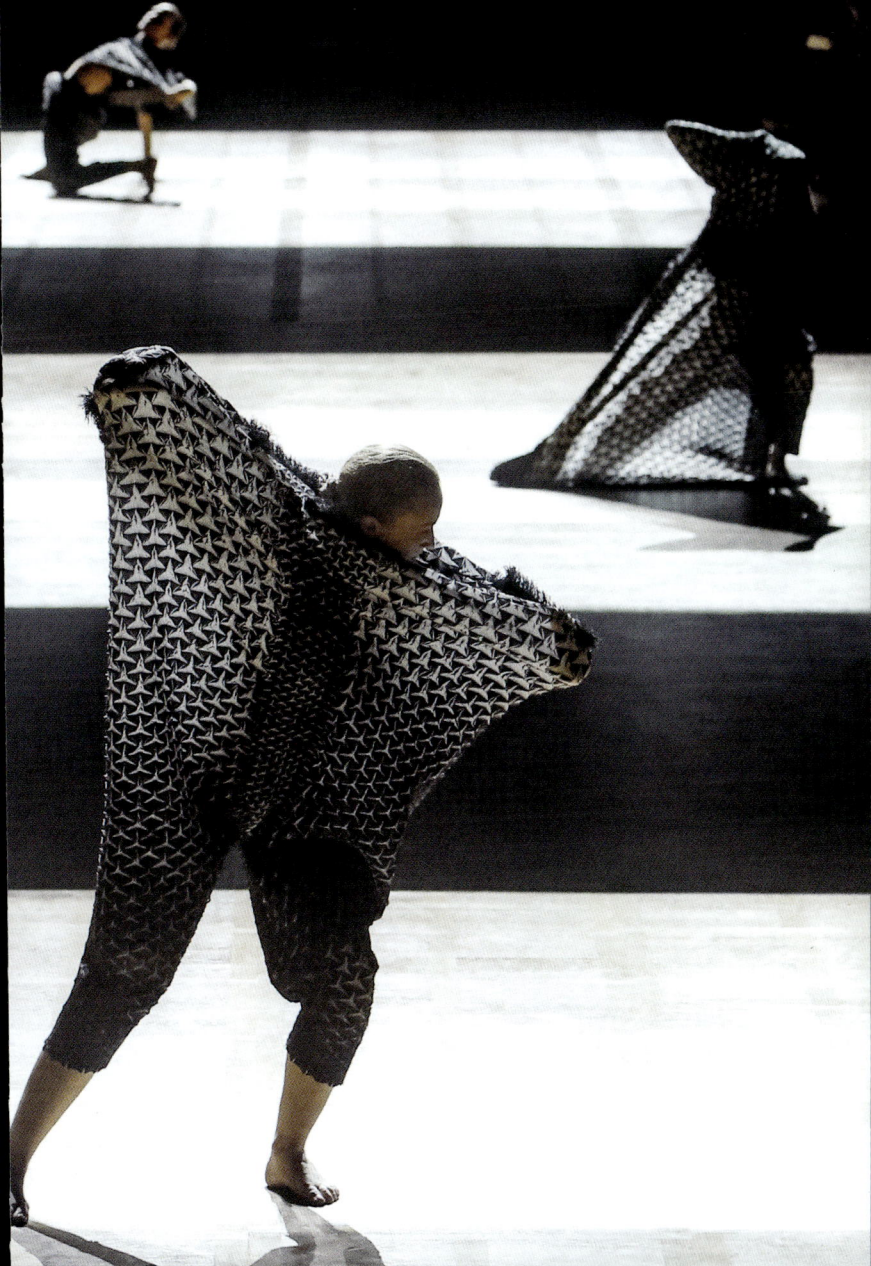

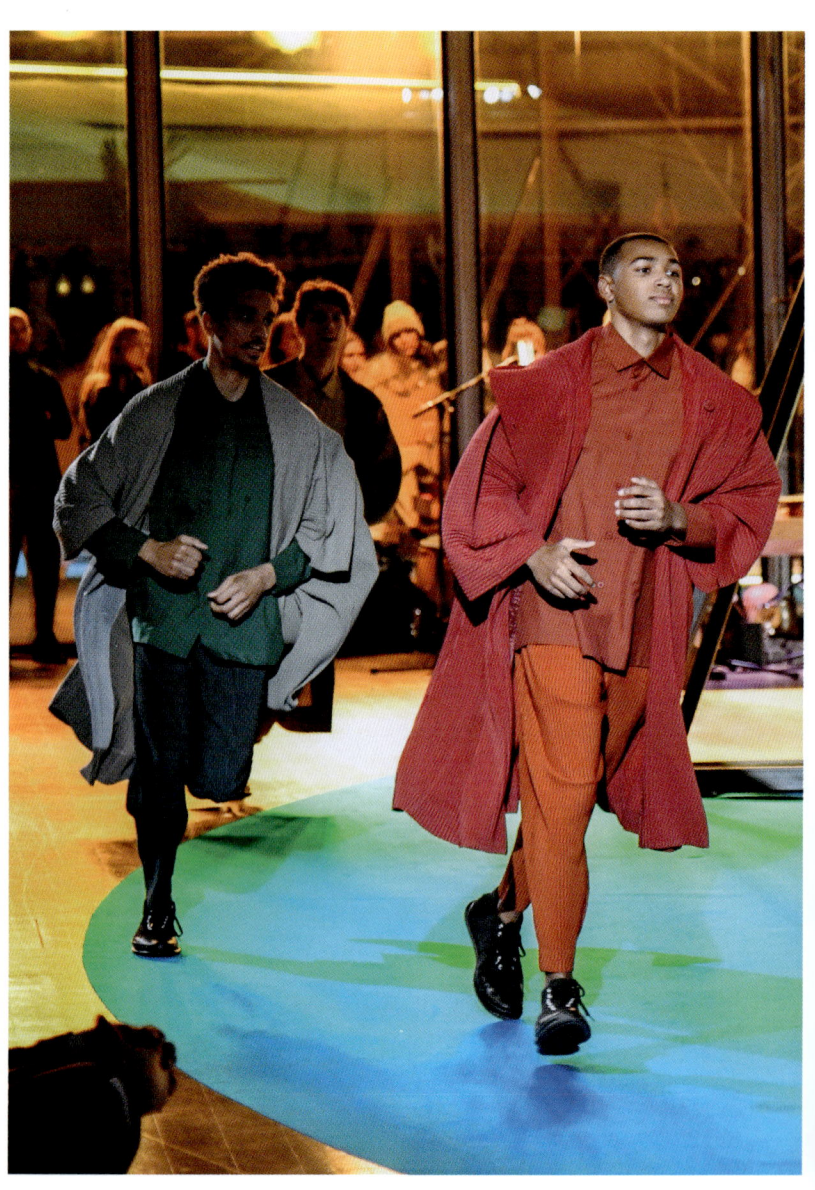

many Pleats disciples from the design and architectural world; others include Frank Gehry, Tadao Ando and Shigeru Ban, with whom Miyake has also collaborated on store designs, installations or products. Zaha Hadid was also an enthusiast of Miyake's designs: one of her favourites was a padded kimono jacket that she preferred to wear upside down.

The late *New York Times* architecture critic Herbert Muschamp, writing on Miyake's sway with this cohort, compared the designer to "a visual philosopher of modern movement, an architect of travelling light."

Muschamp also believed that "if Miyake has attained a position above and beyond fashion, that may be largely because he has given differentiation an architectural shape. Unity,

OPPOSITE Homme Plissé Issey Miyake, A/W 2019.

BELOW From S/S 2020.

OVERLEAF From S/S 2020.

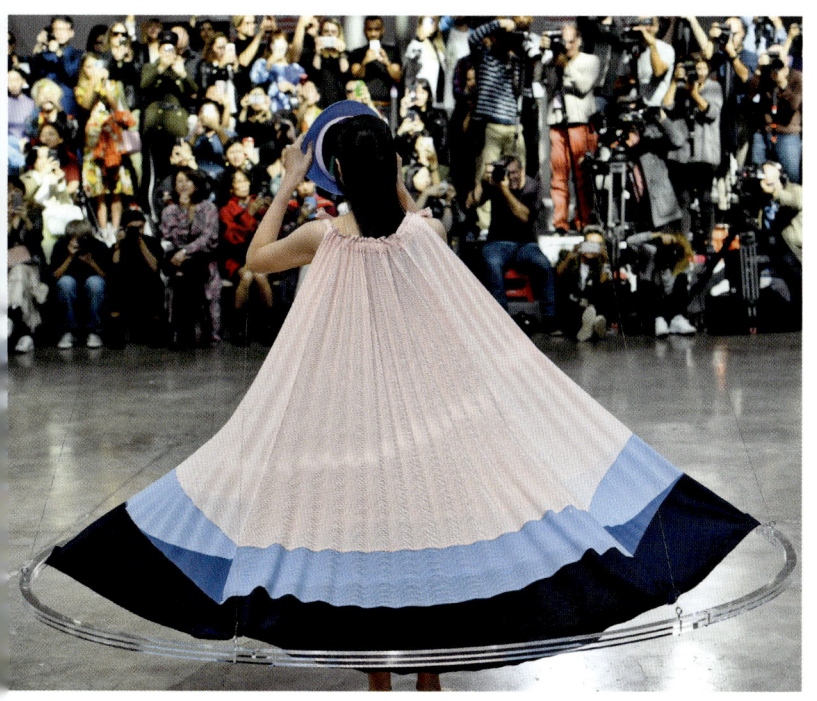

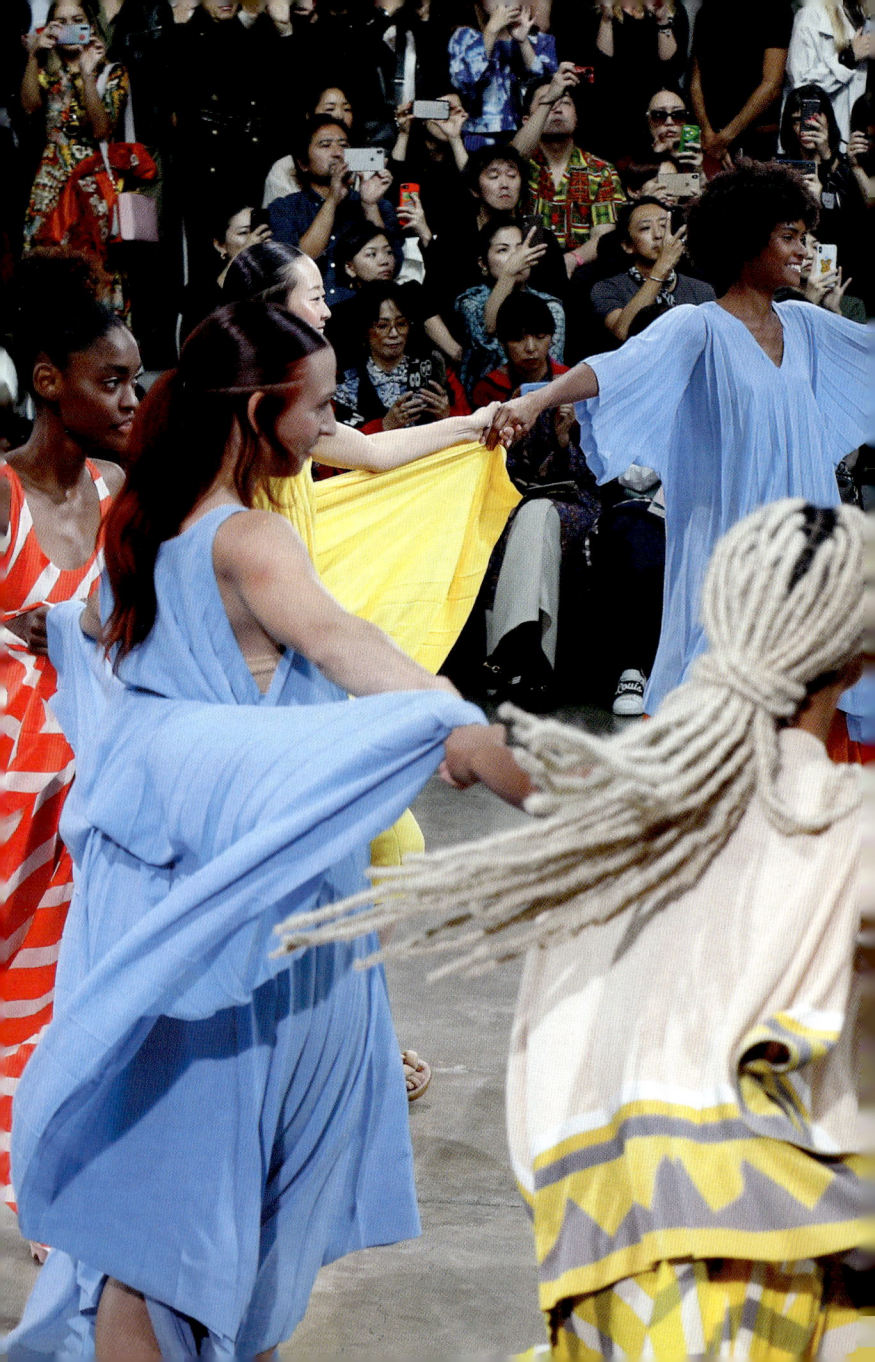

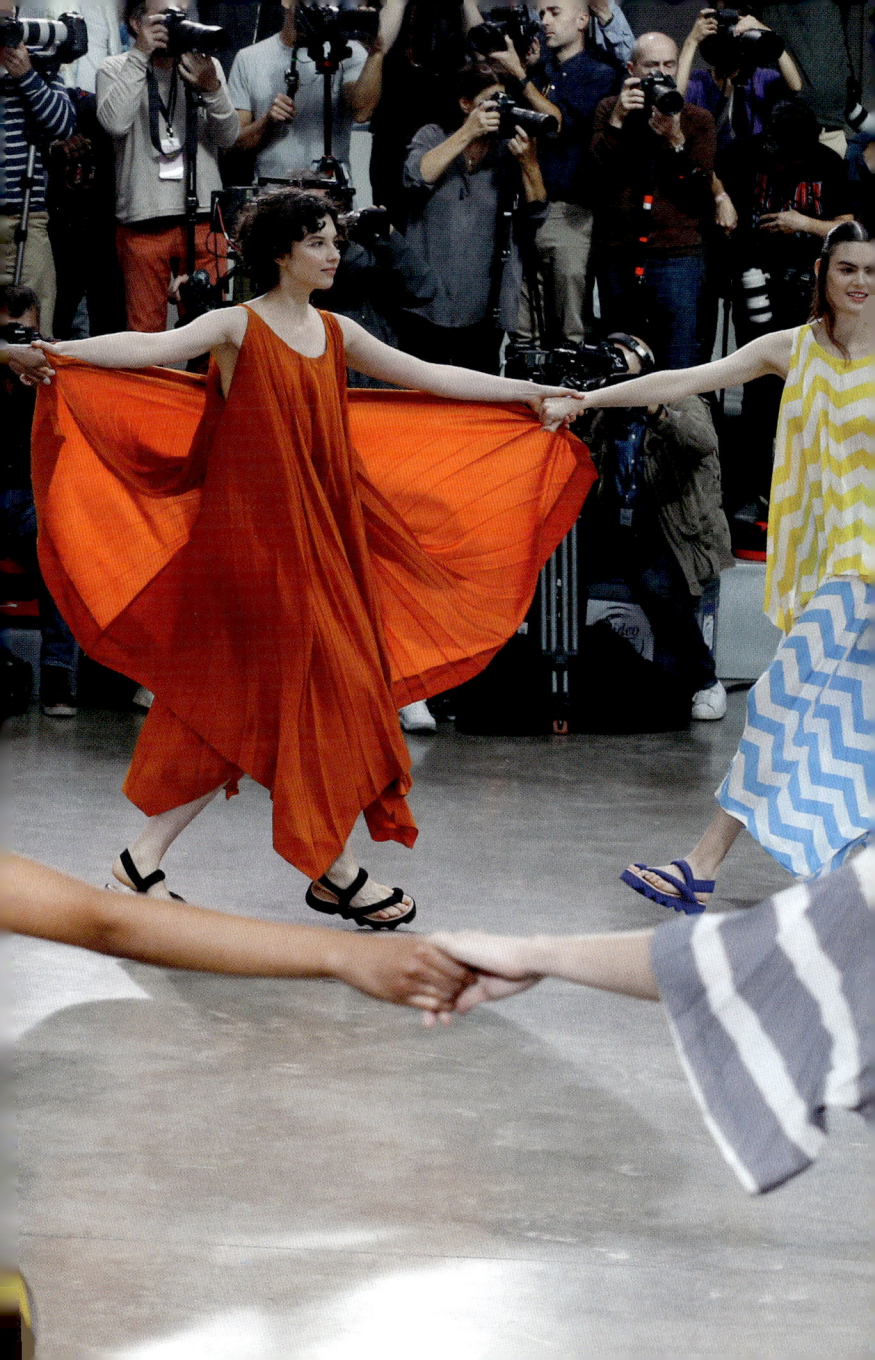

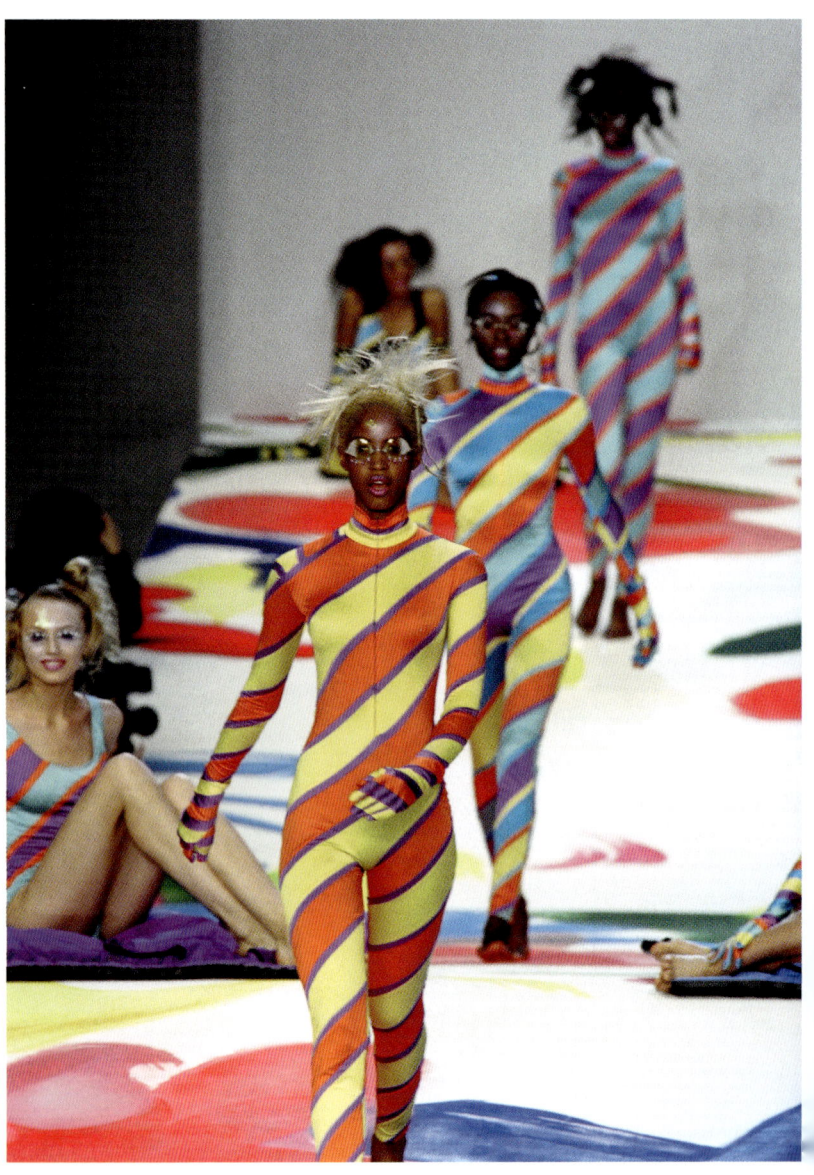

duality, multiplicity: Miyake works with the phenomenon of splitting as if it were a basic law of life, not just a contemporary cultural affliction. He has refined the madness of fashion into a contemplative, creative method, almost a form of meditation on the multiple self."

Although Homme Plissé was only introduced over the past 10 years, Miyake has pushed the creative limits of menswear for decades. His 1991 collection featured knickerbocker trousers with plastic bladders and straws, for men, designed

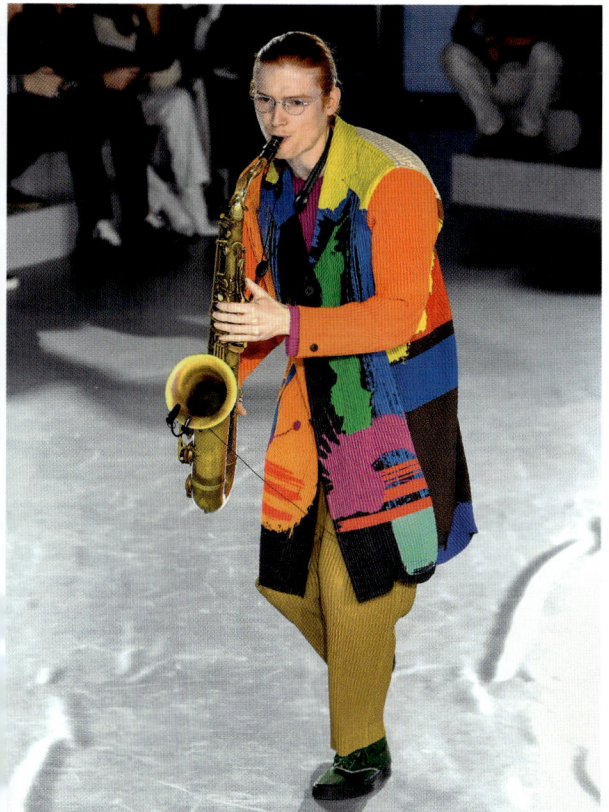

LEFT From A/W 2021.

OPPOSITE Models wear bodysuits covered in spirals of stripes for S/S 1996.

to be inflated or deflated as the wearer wished. Created during the AIDS epidemic, when other brands were producing hyper-masculine clothing and advertising, Miyake saw an opportunity for clothing to "make" one's body and appearance and suit their needs.

OPPOSITE Issey Miyake's fragrance aimed at men, L'Eau d'Issey Pour Homme, launched in 1994.

It's important to note that Miyake was about more than just pleats, or clothing. In 1992, the designer introduced his first and bestselling fragrance L'Eau d'Issey, a lightly sensual floral scent that ended with woody base notes. L'Eau d'Issey was created by French perfumer Jacques Cavallier, its name meaning "Issey's Water" while also being a bilingual pun ("the Odyssey").

The first of a number of perfumes and colognes Miyake would release, it was inspired by water and later instigated a trend for oceanic and marine fragrances.

L'Eau d'Issey's instantly recognizable bottle, in the shape of a slender inverted glass cone topped with a matte silver orb, was designed by Miyake in collaboration with the French art directors Fabien Baron and Alain de Mourgues. Its inspiration was Miyake's observation of the moon rising over the Eiffel Tower in Paris. The year it launched, one bottle was said to have sold every 14 seconds.

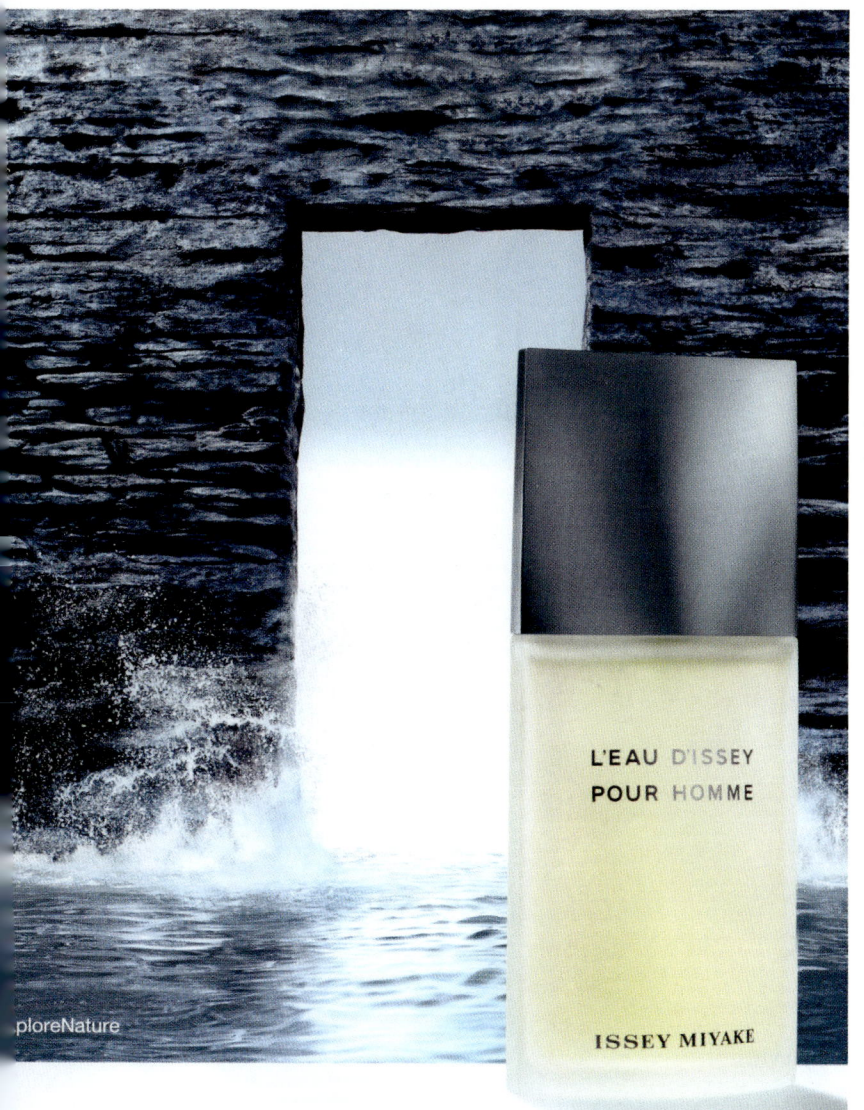

ploreNature

ISSEY MIYAKE
L'EAU D'ISSEY
POUR HOMME

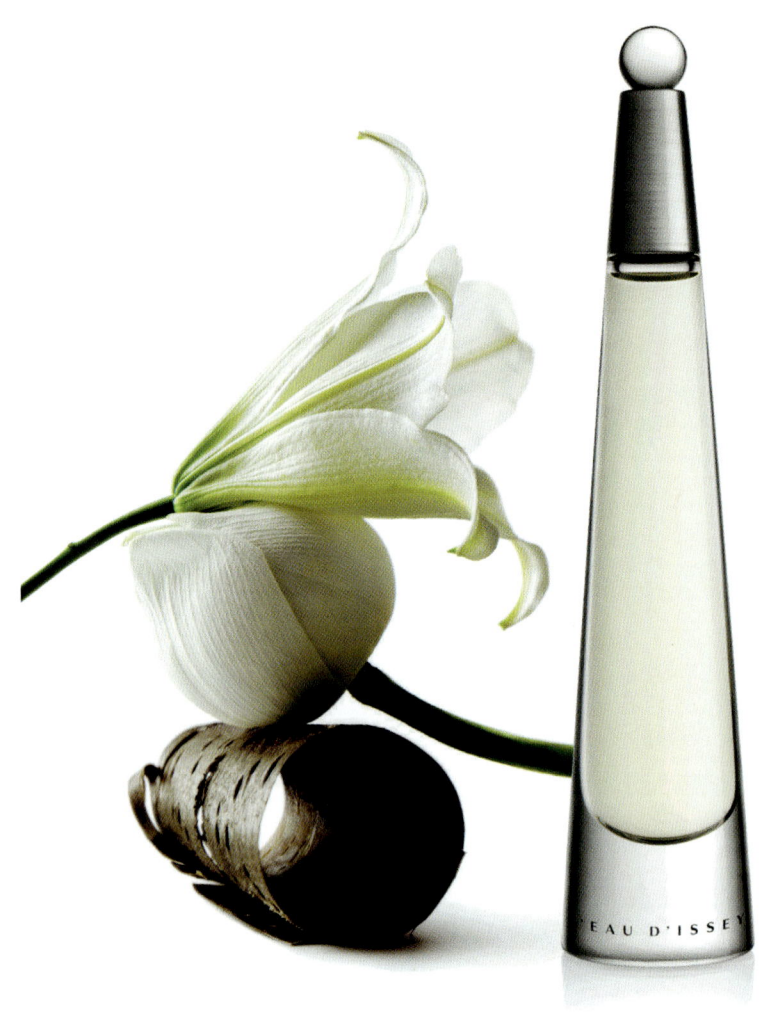

L'EAU D'ISSEY

ISSEY MIYAKE

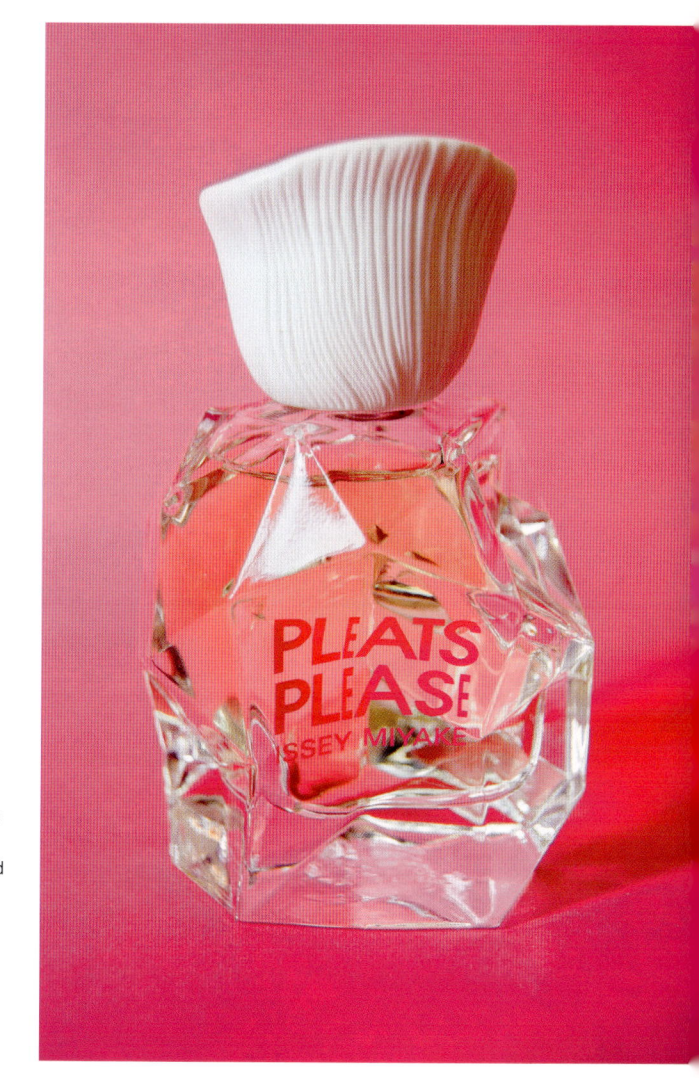

RIGHT Issey Miyake
Pleats Please eau
de toilette launched
in 2013.

OPPOSITE Issey
Miyake's first
fragrance, L'Eau
d'Issey, launched
in 1992

BAO BAO BAGS
AND OTHER
KEY DESIGNS

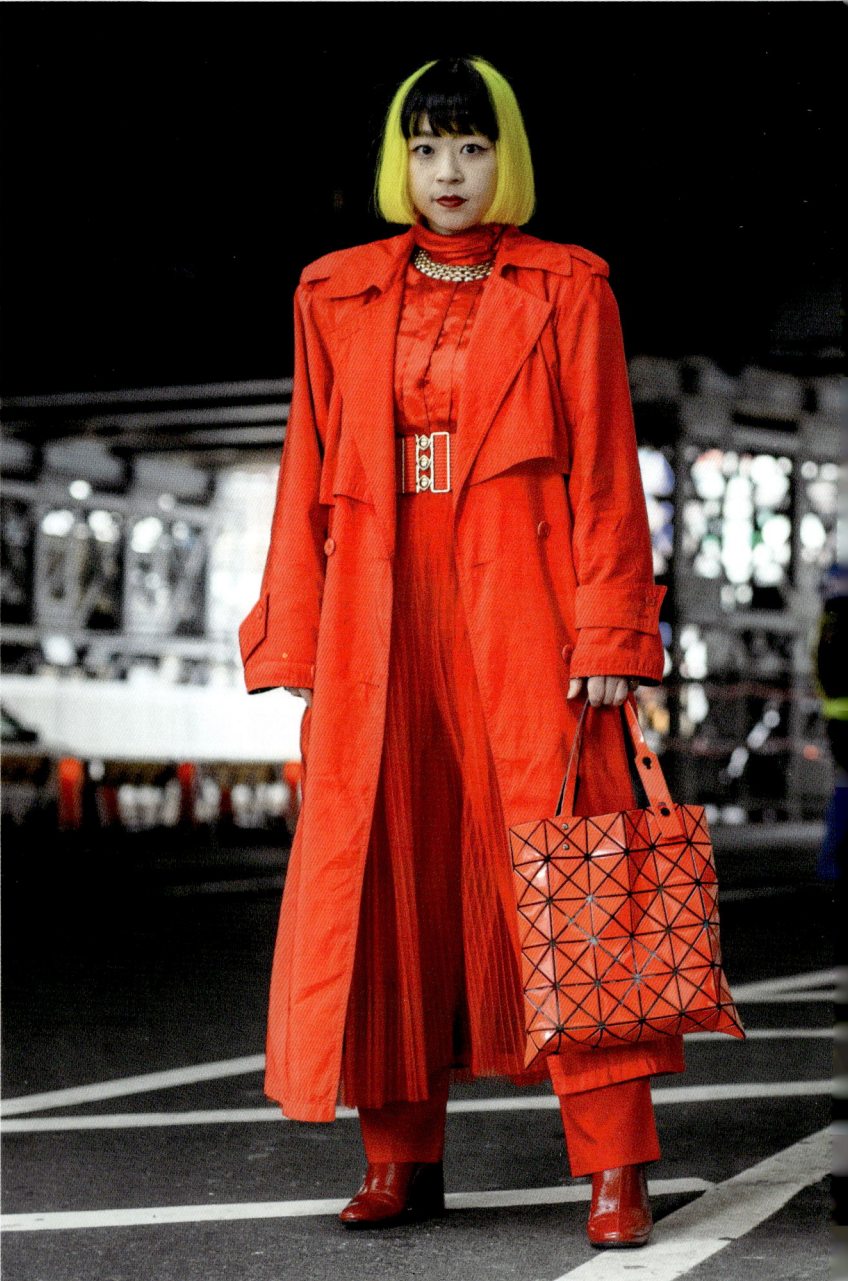

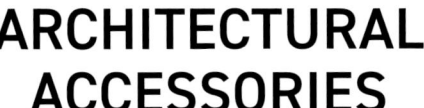

ARCHITECTURAL ACCESSORIES

Another uniquely recognizable design of Miyake's is the Bao Bao bag, which has become an accessory of choice for the creative industries and also now comes in many shapes, sizes and fabric variations.

First released in 2000, it was originally named Bilbao after the Spanish town where the Guggenheim Museum opened in 1997. Designed by Frank Gehry, the landmark was the inspiration for the bag, which is made from small polyvinyl triangles mounted on a mesh fabric underlayer, allowing it to take on different shapes as it is used. The design, intended to create shapes by chance when the bag moved or was placed on various surfaces, marked a continuation of Miyake's experiments with materials and construction.

OPPOSITE A woman in Tokyo carrying an Issey Miyake Bao Bao bag.

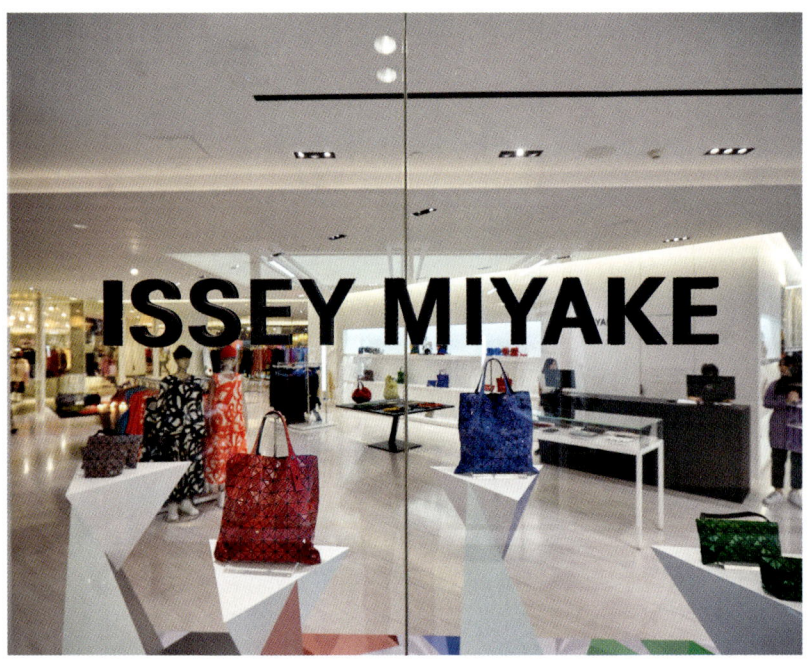

ISSEY MIYAKE

The origami-like style was unlike other versatile bags that were popular around the time, because it was appropriate for the workplace and functional whatever the weather, thanks to its durable, waterproof materials. Priced around £300 to £800, it was also more affordable than many designer bags. The "Bags: Inside Out" exhibition, staged at London's V&A in 2020 and the UK's most comprehensive show dedicated to the ultimate accessory, featured one of Miyake's Bao Bao bags in a lucent metallic colour.

Such is the enduring popularity of the Bao Bao that there are now dedicated stores globally, in countries such as Japan and China. In 2016, Miyake expanded its range beyond the iconic triangular pieces, with the launch of the Chord

ABOVE An Issey Miyake store selling Bao Bao bags.

OPPOSITE A new bag is presented at the show for S/S 2017.

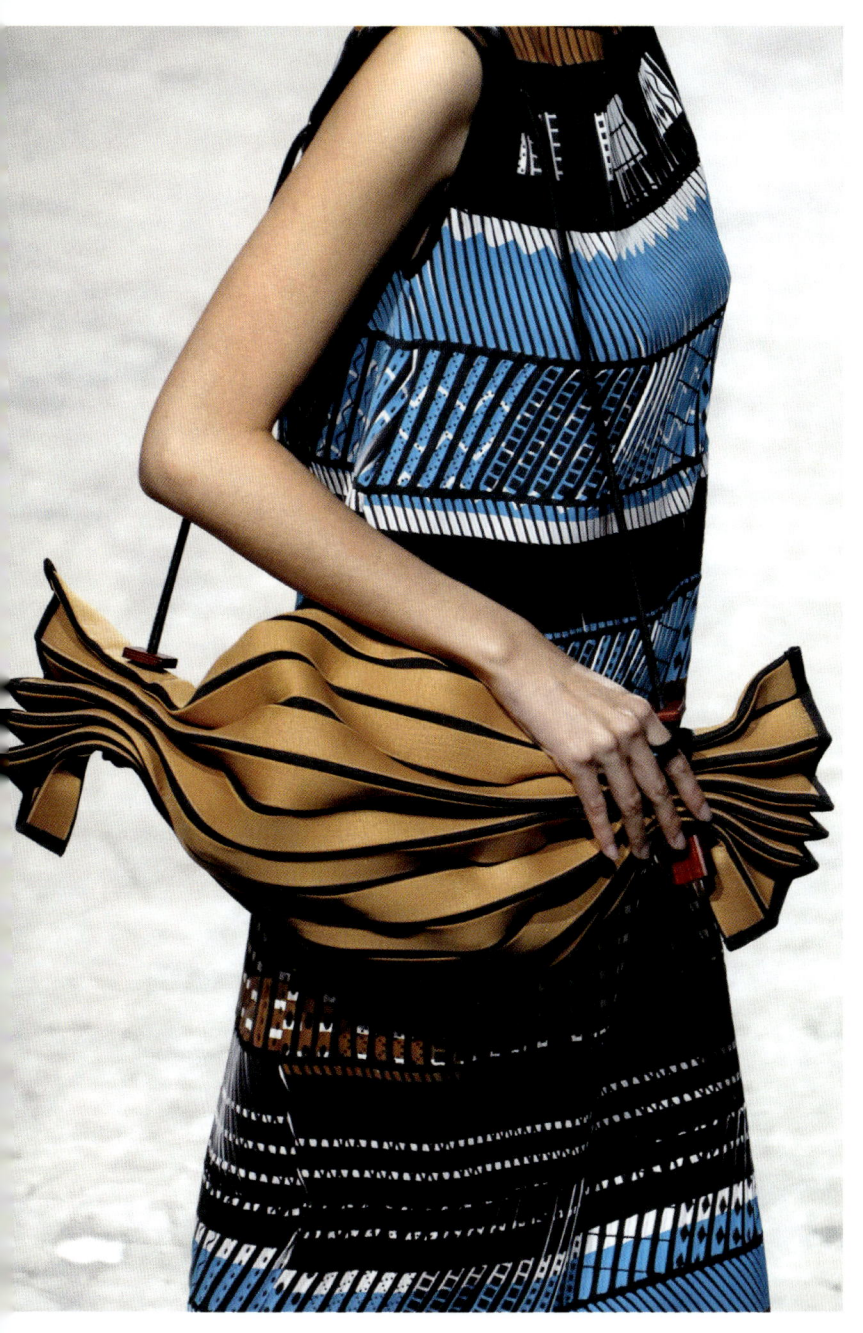

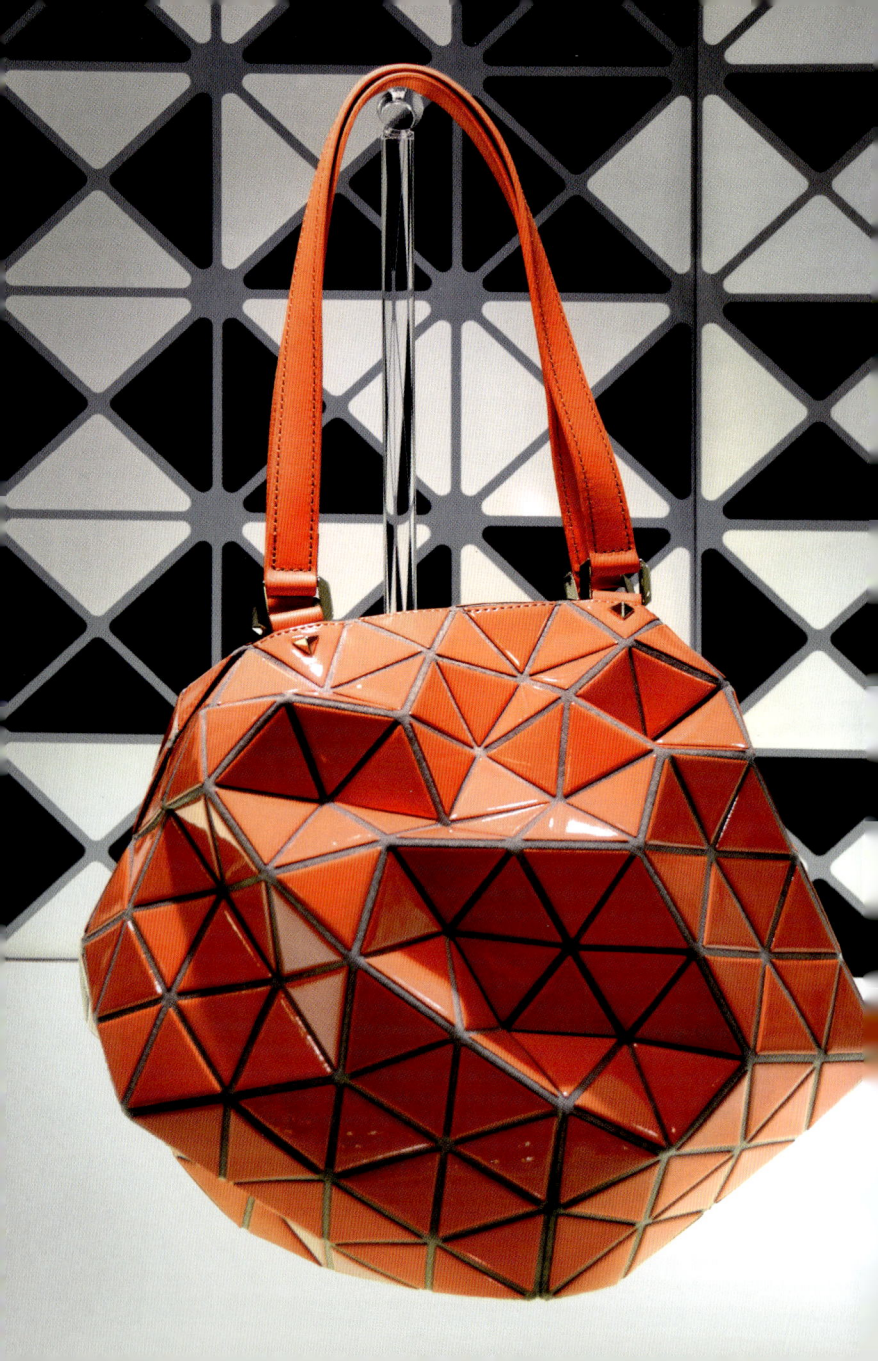

OPPOSITE Issey Miyake's Bao Bao bag in orange.

BELOW Carrying Issey Miyake's Bao Bao bag in yellow.

collection featuring a multitude of shapes (including round and square details), some even featuring prints. In 2020, the brand introduced a miniature version of its signature geometric style, called the Hello Bao Bao bag, for its 20th anniversary.

In 2022, Miyake introduced one of its most technically advanced approaches to accessories with the introduction of "Dazzle", a new series of Bao Bao bags composed from puzzle-like pieces that create theoretically endless combinations when slotted together (much like the original aim of the Bao Bao, to create infinite and versatile shapes).

The bag pieces, each identical in shape, are created using a high-precision moulding technique. The result is a structured exterior, even while the bag retains its light feel and slouchy shape. The idea behind the Dazzle design was that singular pieces could be replaced if they become damaged or worn, offering a sustainable and affordable alternative to replacing the entire bag. For a limited period, the brand also offered a

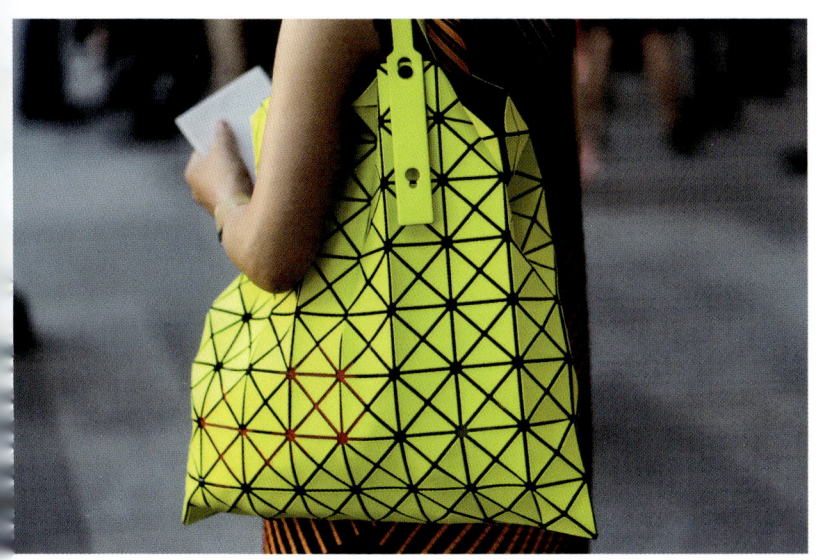

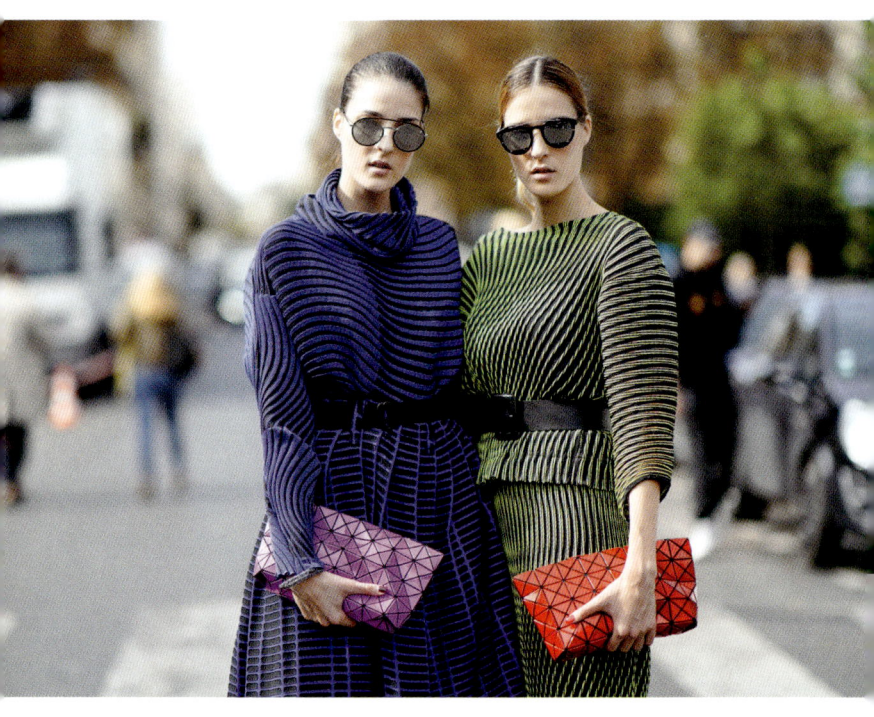

ABOVE Two women
dressed in purple
and green striped
Issey Miyake
dresses, carrying
Issey Miyake's Bao
Bao bags.

customizable service where unique colour combinations could be pre-ordered.

Other lesser known but equally inventive collections by Miyake include HaaT, a women's ready-to-wear brand, launched in 2000, which is inspired by textile innovation and led by Miyake's former textile designer Makiko Minagawa, who worked beside Issey Miyake for over three decades. HaaT's aim, according to the brand, is to ennoble traditional craftsmanship and natural materials from across Japan and India, and to be worn across "modern diverse lifestyles". Its name plays on the word "market" in Sanskrit and intentionally sounds similar to "heart" in English.

HaaT uses *Kyo chijimi* fabrics; these are woven by artisans in Japan's Shiga Prefecture and gaps are left in the thread to minimize contact between fabric and skin, which allows the garment to adapt to different temperatures. It is then passed through natural spring water, which shrinks the fabric and produces its signature earthy hues. Other garments from the range are handcrafted in India, in the city of Ahmedabad, a relationship made possible by Minagawa's long-standing admiration for the country's materials and techniques. (The designer played her part in a commission from the Indian government in 1983 to make clothes using Indian materials; the result of the collaboration was later exhibited at the Musée des Arts Décoratifs in Paris as part of France's "Year of India" cultural programme.)

In 2001, Miyake launched Cauliflower, a one-size shirt that stretches to fit the wearer, while Issey Miyake Fete, a colourful women's line that draws on the technological innovations of Pleats Please, was launched in 2004. That year, he also established The Miyake Issey Foundation, which holds archives of his work. It also runs a design and fashion training programme aimed at creating the young professionals of the future.

In 2007, the foundation opened an exhibition centre in Tokyo, which stages shows themed around Japanese design. Miyake was appointed its director, along with graphic designer Taku Satoh, author Naoto Fukasawa and engineer Noriko Kawakami.

In 2020, Miyake debuted 132 5., an eco-friendly line made from recycled materials. By then, he had stepped back from the day-to-day running of his brands but still remained involved. Miyake's in-house research and development team, founded in 2007 and known as Reality Lab, was inspired by the work of computer scientist Jun Mitani, who creates three-dimensional structures by folding flat materials. Together they worked on the development of the garments, which expanded from two-dimensional geometric shapes into structural dresses and separates including shirts, trousers and skirts.

Miyake was decorated for his efforts in nearly every field he worked in: he received the Wexner Prize (given to contemporary artists whose work has been consistently original, influential and challenging to convention) in 2004 and Japan's international art prize, the Praemium Imperiale in the category of sculpture in 2005, lauding him for his exploration of the relationship between clothing and the human body. The following year, Miyake was awarded the Arts and Philosophy Kyoto Prize, Japan's most prestigious private prize, for lifetime achievement in the arts. In 2010, he was awarded Japan's Order of Culture, the country's highest arts honour, and in 2014, Italy's industrial design award, Compasso d'Oro. Tokyo's National Art Center honoured Miyake with a retrospective in 2016.

OPPOSITE A model wears an origami-inspired design, created by Dai Fujiwara.

OVERLEAF Models wearing origami-inspired designs, created by Dai Fujiwara, for A/W 2021.

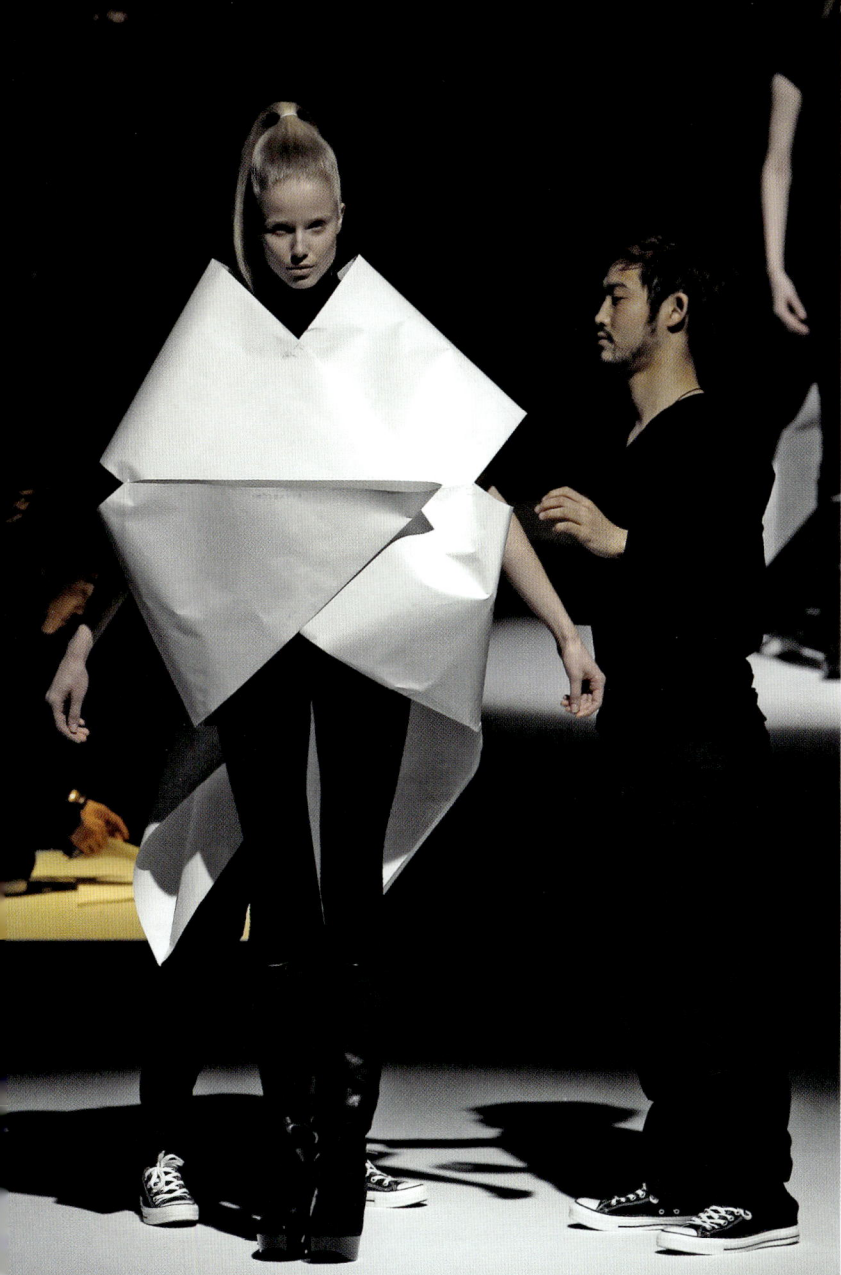

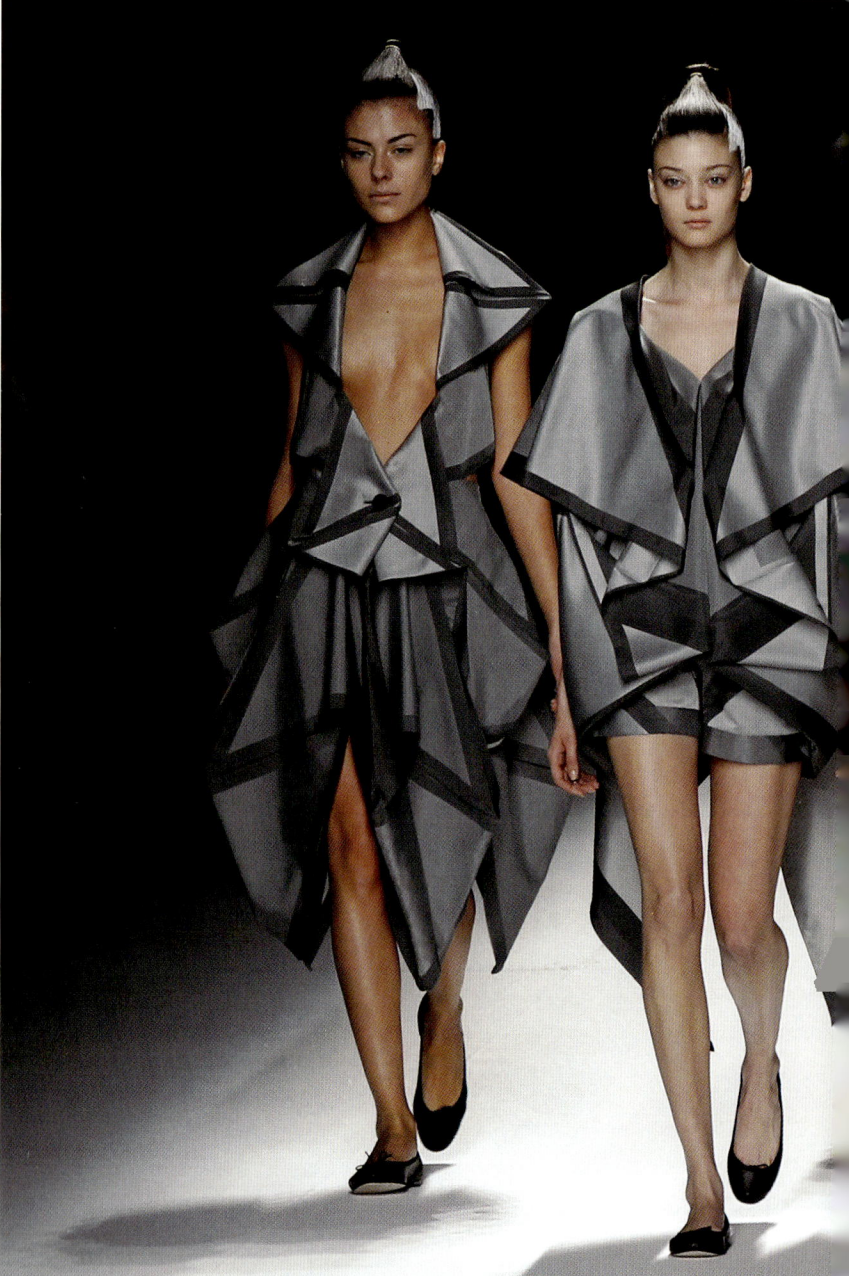

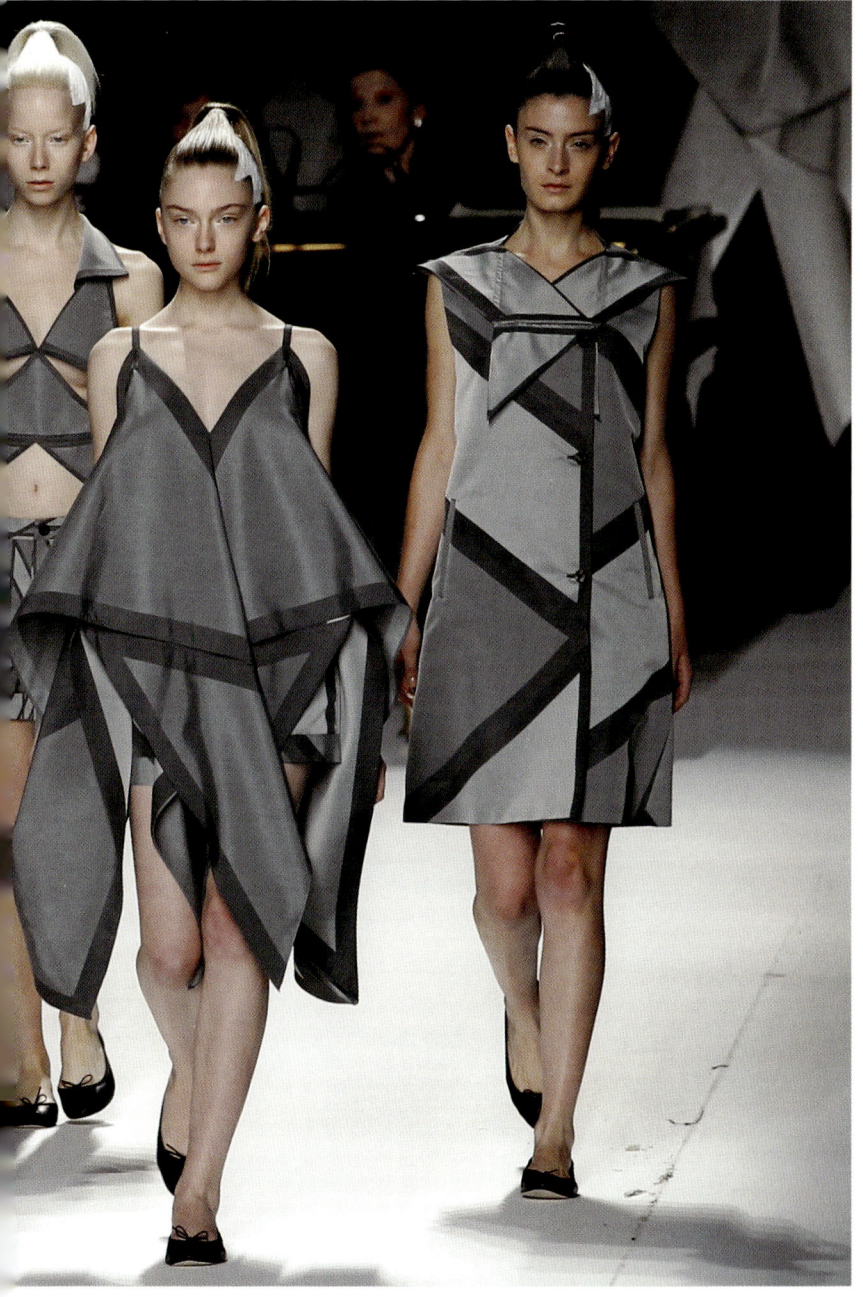

ENDURING INFLUENCE

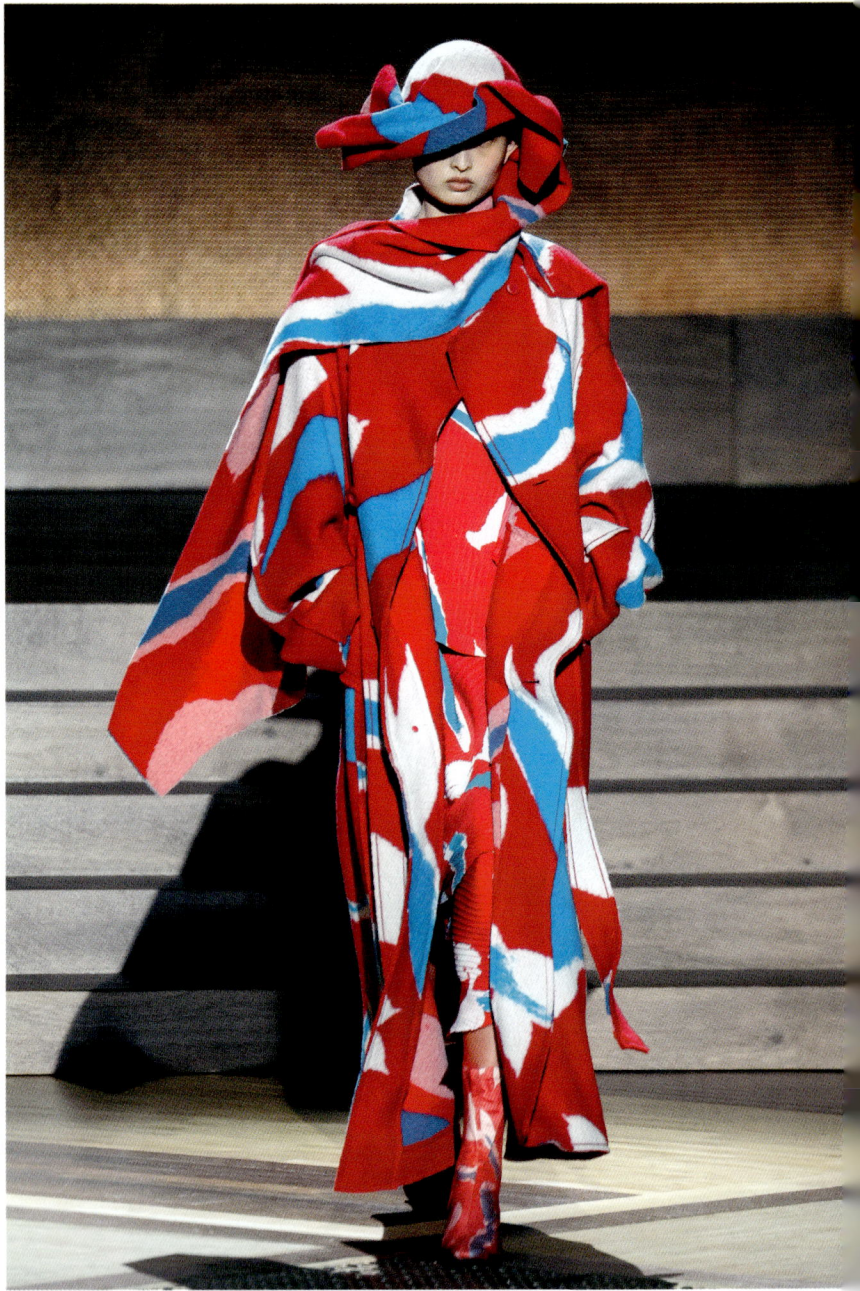

IMPACT ON THE FASHION LANDSCAPE

Miyake formally retired from fashion in 1997 but continued to oversee the creative direction of all the lines created by his company until his death in 2022, aged 84.

F ollowing Miyake's retirement, the reins were handed over to Naoki Takizawa, a Tokyo native, who helped design the brand's Plantation collection in 1983, using mostly natural materials and featuring simple, loose designs that were easy to care for. Takizawa formally joined the Issey Miyake design team in 1989 and became creative director, overseeing Issey Miyake's menswear and womenswear, in 1999.

In 2006 Takizawa established his own studio and was succeeded as creative director by Dai Fujiwara, who oversaw the creative direction for five years, until 2011. The design duties for the Spring/Summer 2012 collections were divided by Yoshiyuki Miyamae, head designer of the women's collection who had joined the Miyake Design Studio in 2001 and was a member of the original team that developed A-POC, and Bunka Fashion University graduate Yusuke Takahashi, who designed the men's line.

OPPOSITE From A/W 2024.

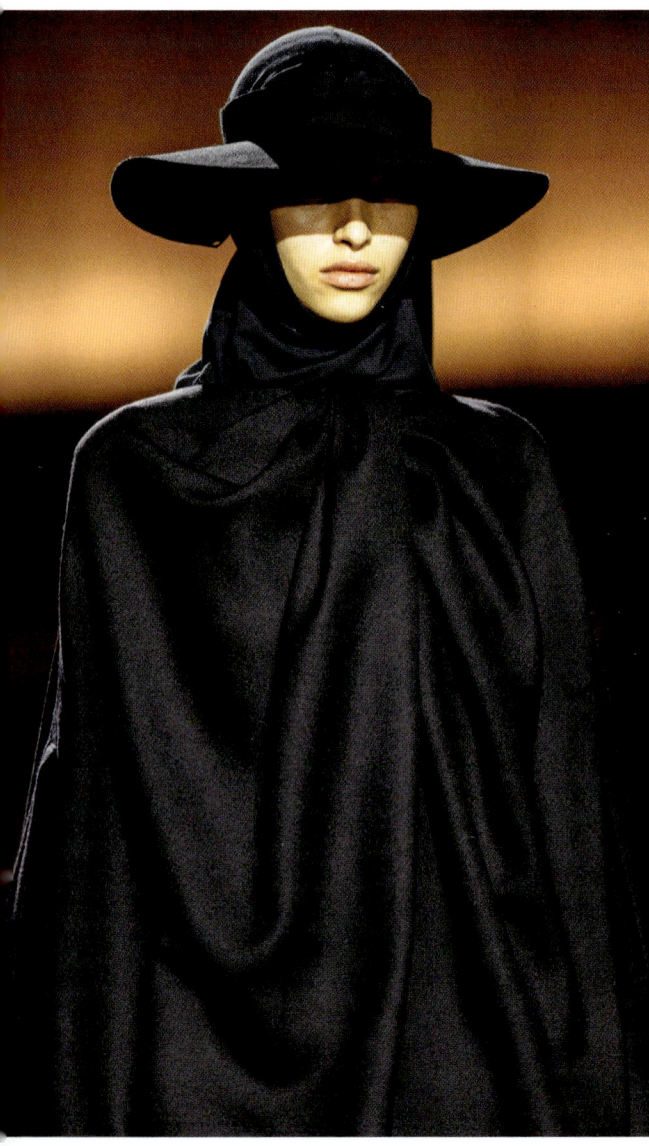

LEFT AND OPPOSITE From A/W 2024.

OVERLEAF Menswear A/W 2024.

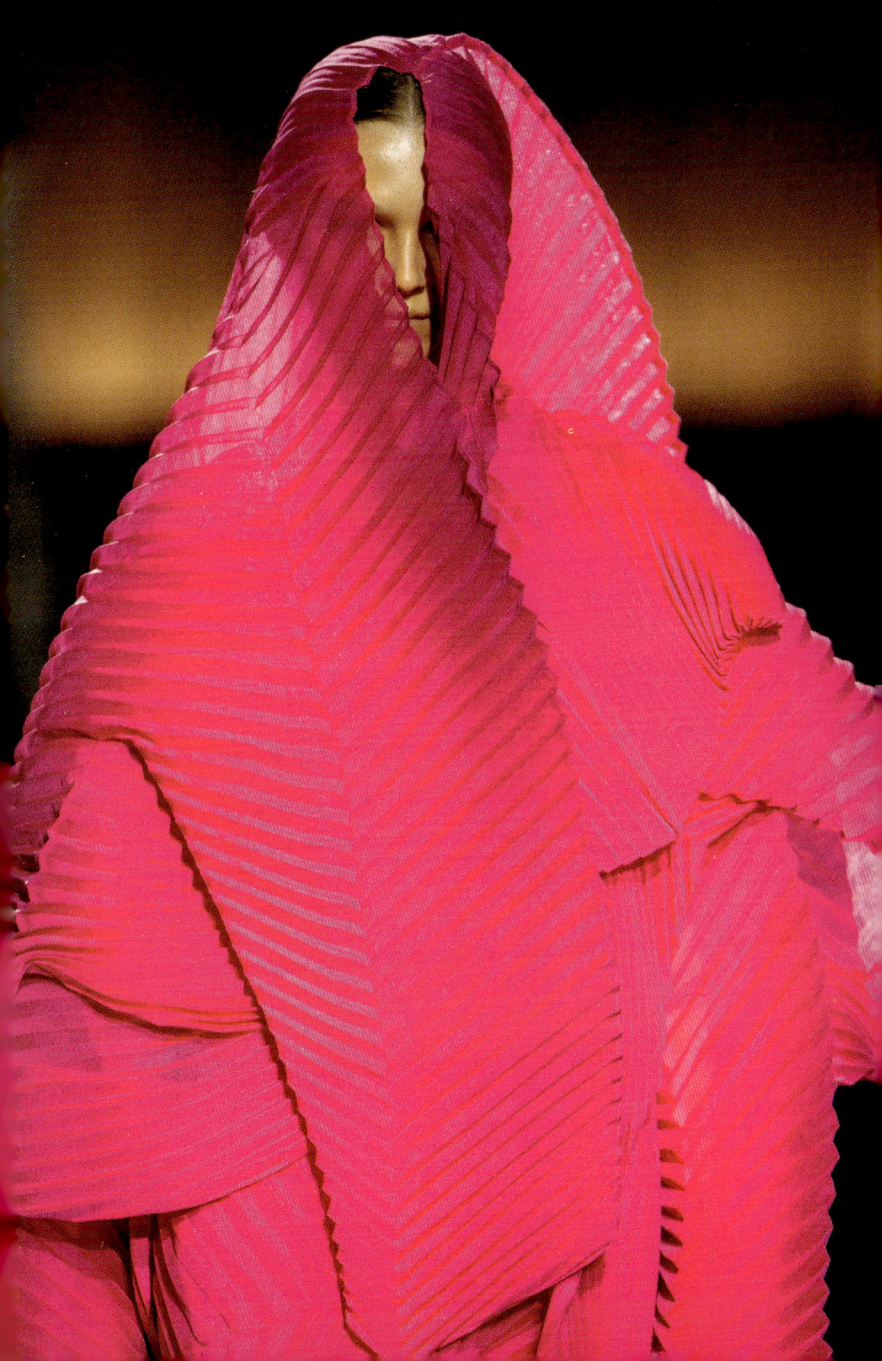

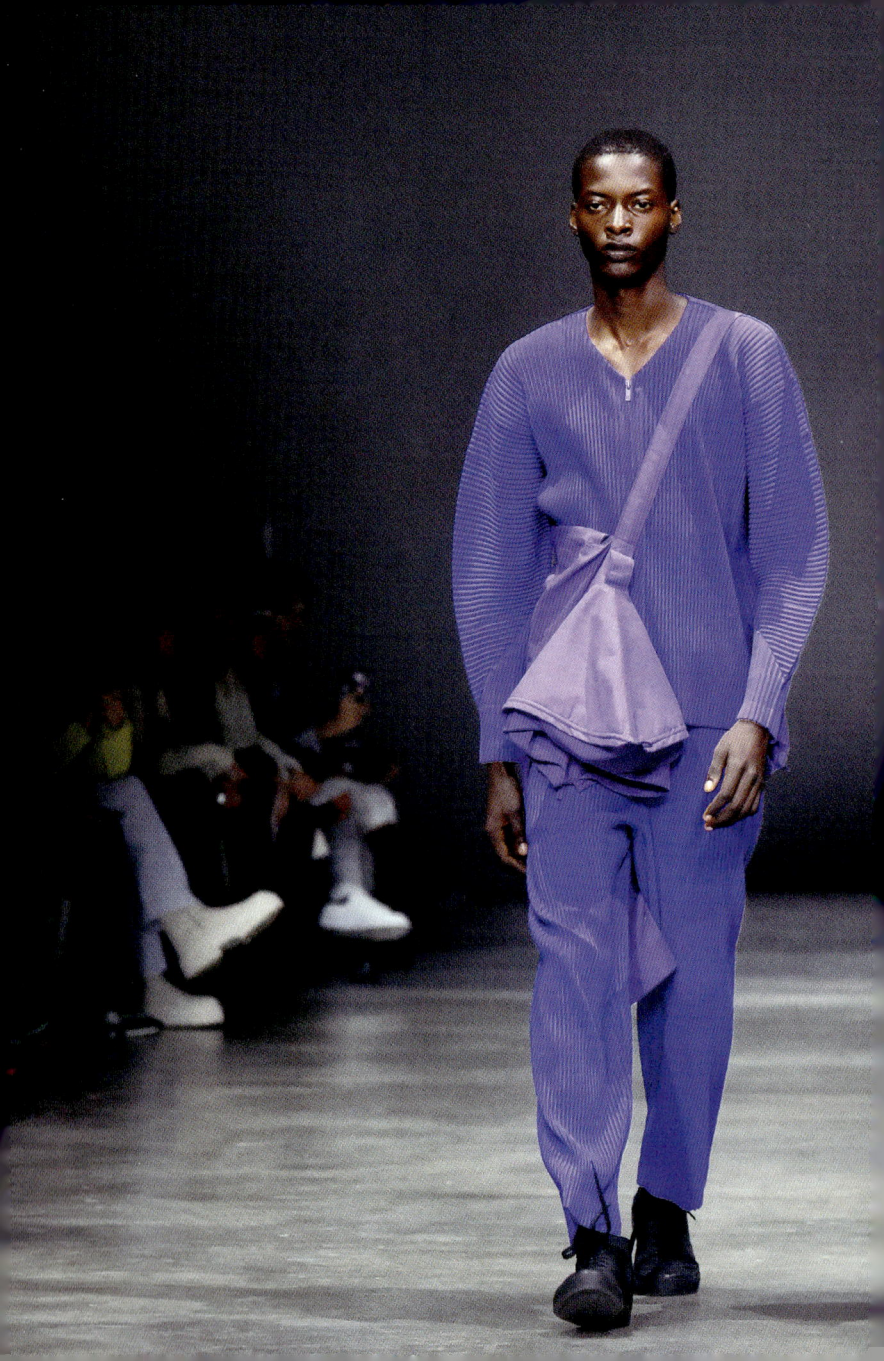

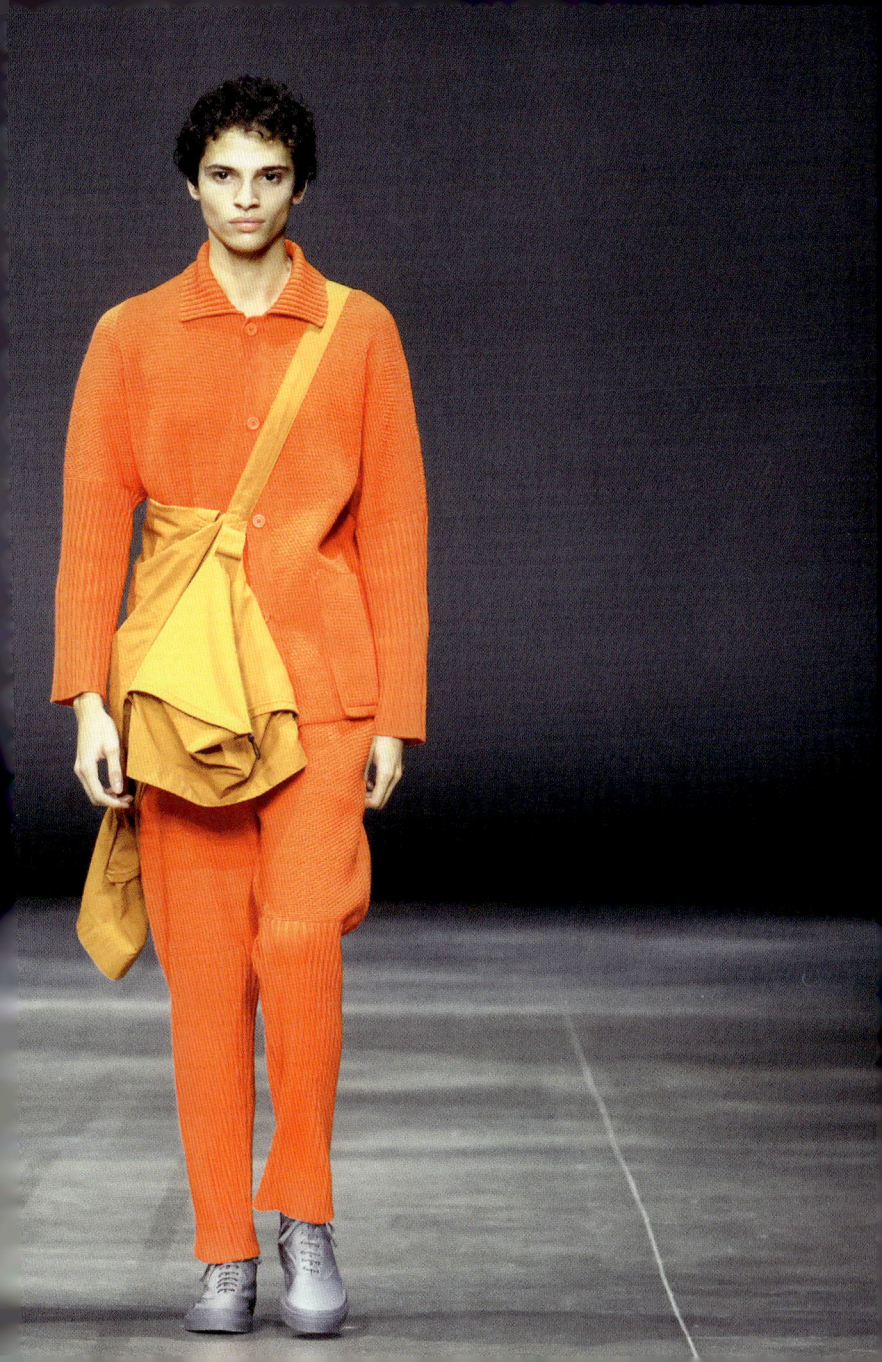

Designer Satoshi Kondo, who had worked with Miyake over many years in roles at Pleats Please and Homme Plissé, was named as creative director of Issey Miyake in 2019. His first collection for the house, for Spring/Summer 2020, was presented through choreography that included skateboarding, running and skipping by models, dancers, acrobats and even musicians, to demonstrate the clothing's propensity for movement. Outfits descended from the ceiling right onto the models, who waited with their arms stretched up, like children who were being dressed by an adult. There was a clear love for colour and geometry in the clothes, which stretched, expanded and bounced perfectly, as each model moved around joyously.

In 2020, when most people were housebound due to the pandemic, Miyake's pleated designs developed a new ardent

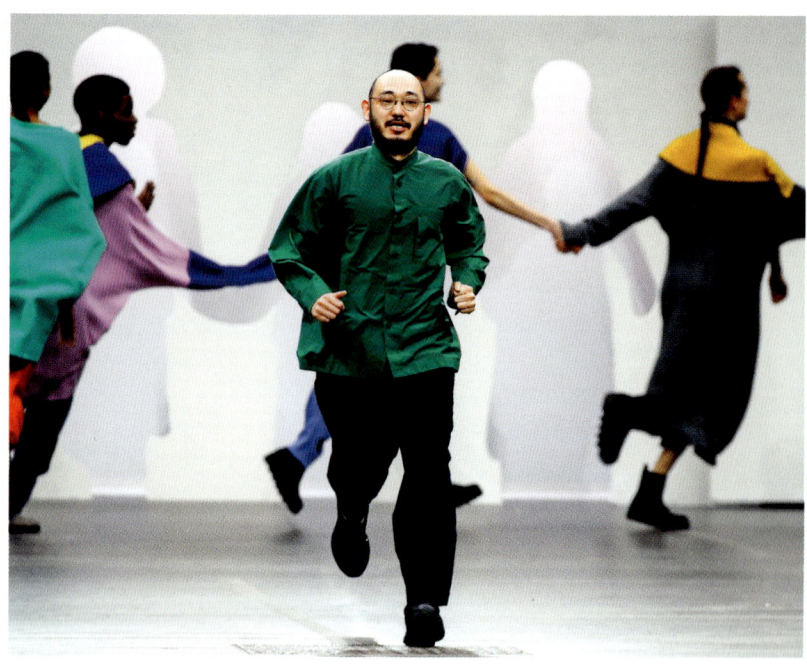

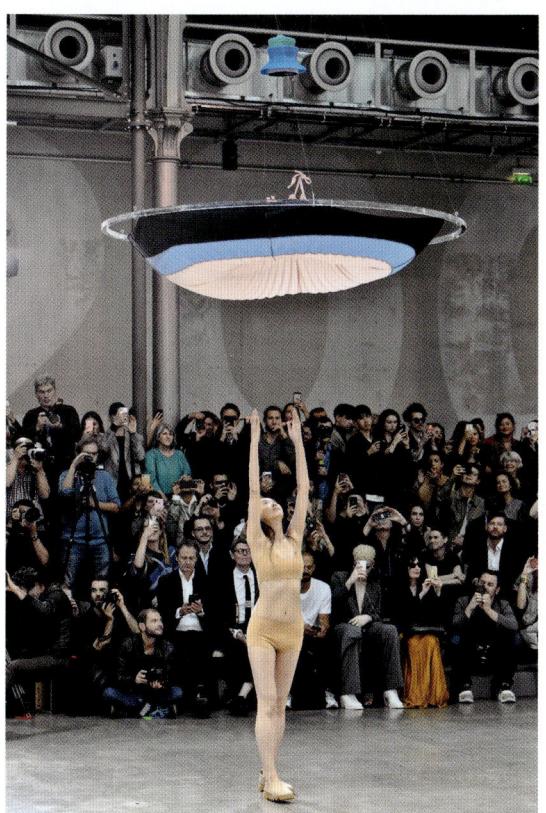

RIGHT Models were dressed on the runway during the show for S/S 2020.

OVERLEAF Menswear S/S 2023.

following. Younger customers, in search of comfortable clothing that could be worn and looked after with ease, had now discovered the brand.

Two years later, in August 2022, Miyake passed away. The Miyake Design Studio said the cause was liver cancer. The day his death was announced, an outpouring of tributes from around the world splashed across social media, illustrating just how many people wore and engaged with the designer's work.

The Spring/Summer 2023 show, the first collection to be shown since Miyake's death, focused on shaping garments,

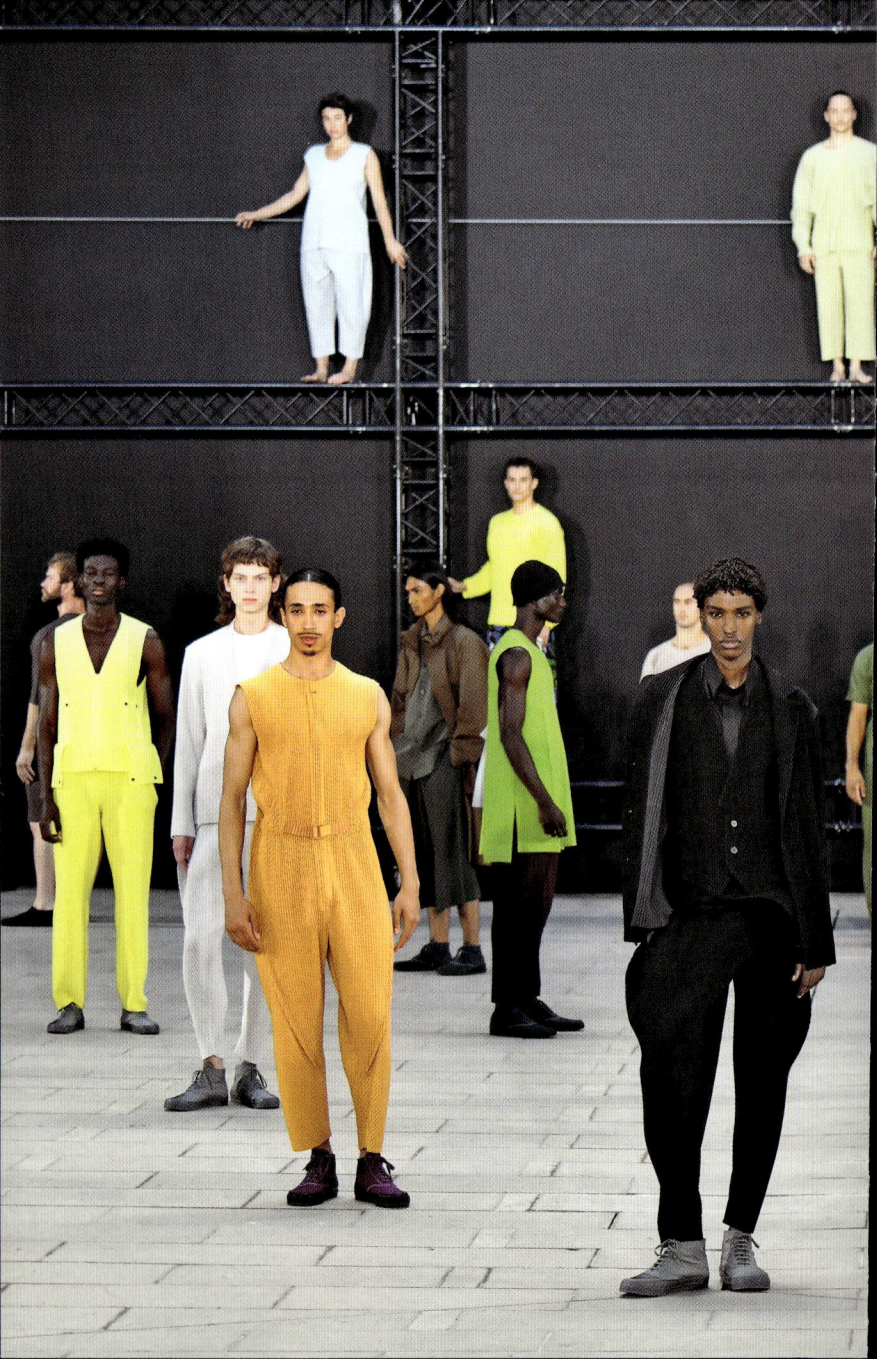

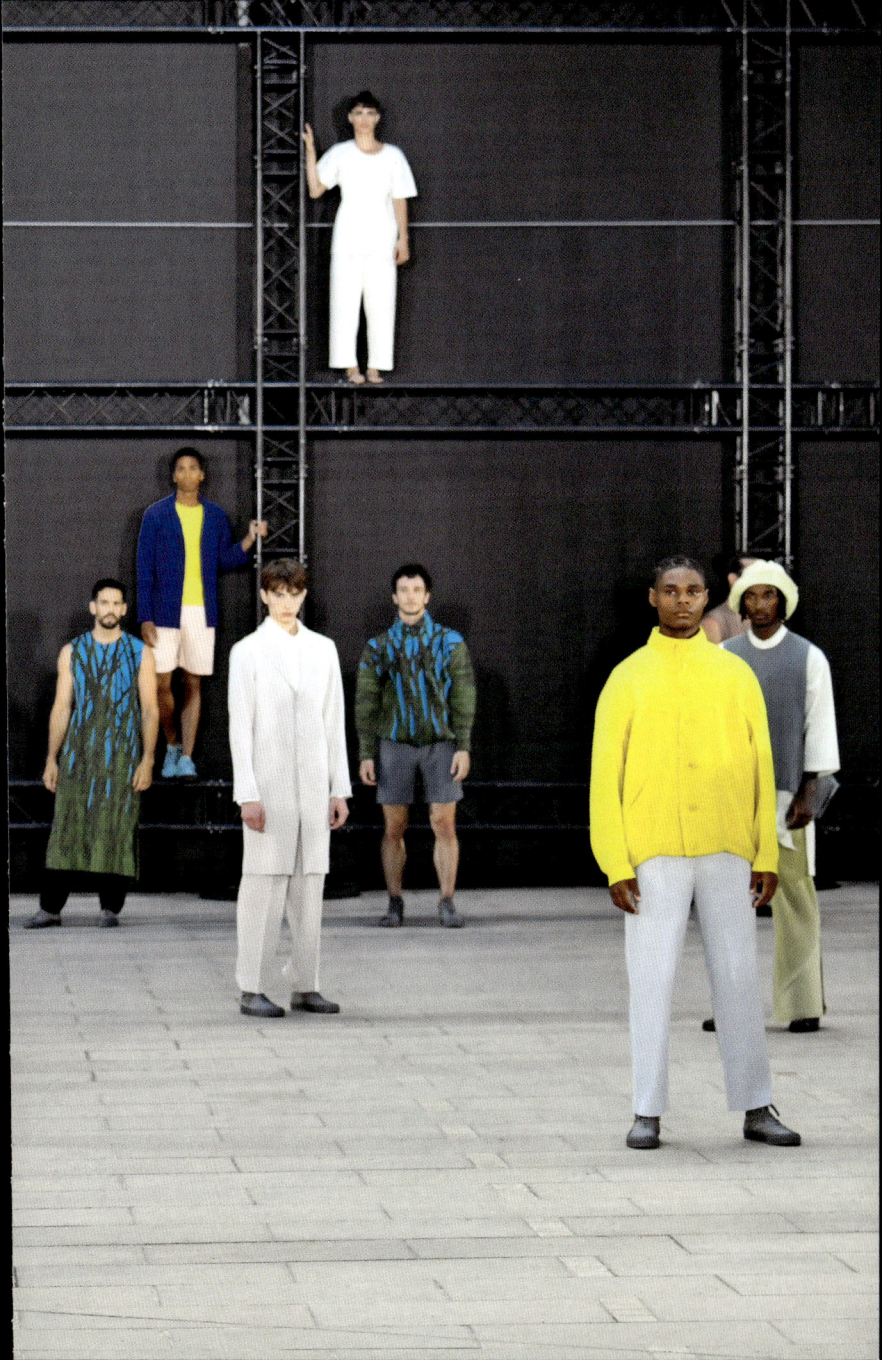

inspired by Miyake's own command of body and silhouette. "Every collection I created with my team is a reflection of what we learned from Miyake," Kondo told *Wallpaper* magazine. "Moving forward, as we have always done in the past, we will challenge ourselves to create original, unprecedented clothing that brings a sense of joy and wonder, building upon what is true to the brand's identity."

On each of the seats at the show was a piece of *washi* paper, a traditional Japanese material that is processed by hand using fibres of the gampi tree or mulberry bush, and which has been utilized for more than a thousand years as a fabric for clothing, particularly in northern Japan. (Such is *washi*'s cultural importance that UNESCO recognizes it as intangible cultural heritage.)

Embossed with reflective words from Kondo and the team, the paper served as a tribute to Miyake, who during his lifetime had been captivated by the functionality of *washi* and used it in his collections, mixed with polyester or cotton to create innovative new fabrications. Of course, Miyake's fascination with *washi* also spoke to his general approach of marrying the traditional and modern, and science with innovation.

Over the course of his career, Miyake attracted a large following of celebrities who mostly had nothing in common other than their enthusiasm for wearing Issey Miyake. That ranged from actor Robin Williams, who was photographed in 1997 wearing his Issey Miyake bomber to the premiere of *Flubber* in New York, to singer-songwriter Solange, who in 2019 performed on *The Tonight Show Starring Jimmy Fallon* wearing interconnected jumpsuits created by her mom Tina, inspired by a 1999 Miyake design.

Miyake's designs have always appeared to attract those who love design more than fashion, but among his biggest fans was the legendary fashion critic Suzy Menkes, who has become

OPPOSITE Robin Williams attends the *Flubber* premiere in New York, 1997, wearing an Issey Miyake bomber jacket.

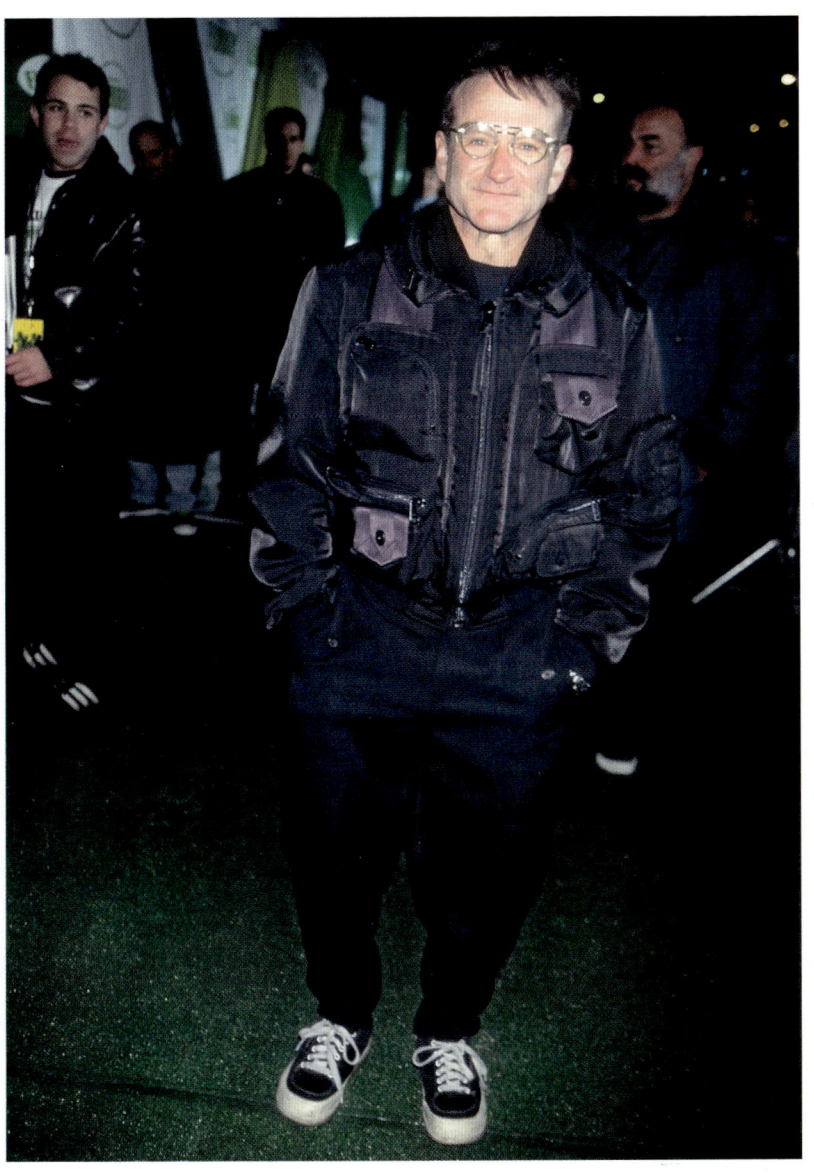

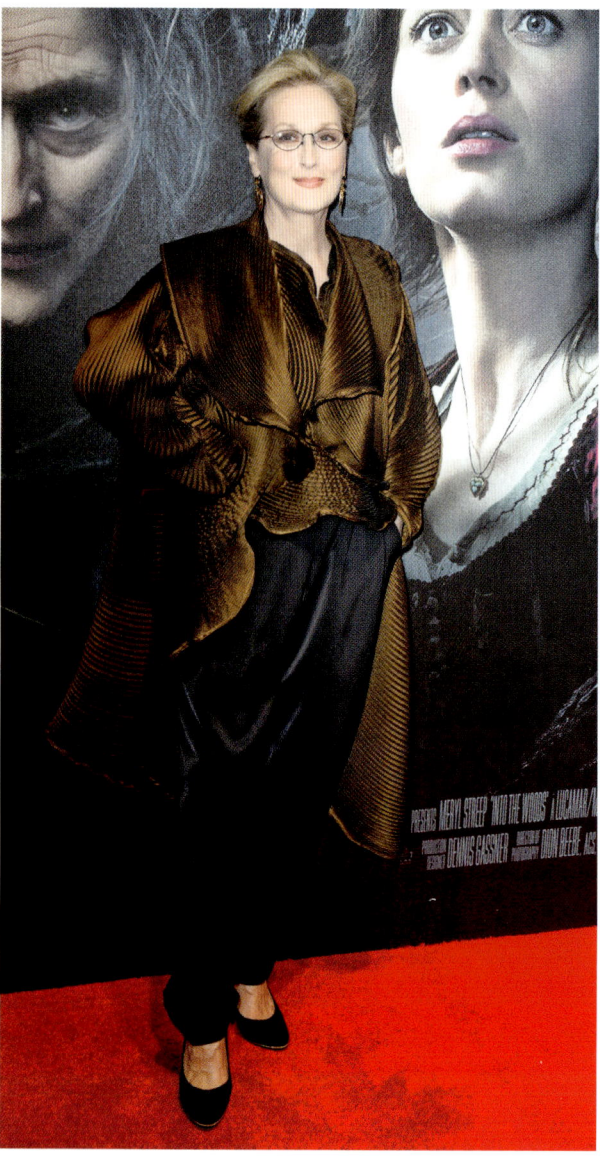

LEFT Meryl Streep wears Issey Miyake to the UK screening of *Into the Woods* in London.

OPPOSITE Cynthia Nixon (wearing a dress from S/S 2023), Kristin Davis and Sarah Jessica Parker attend a private celebration to celebrate the 25th anniversary of *Sex and the City*, held in New York City.

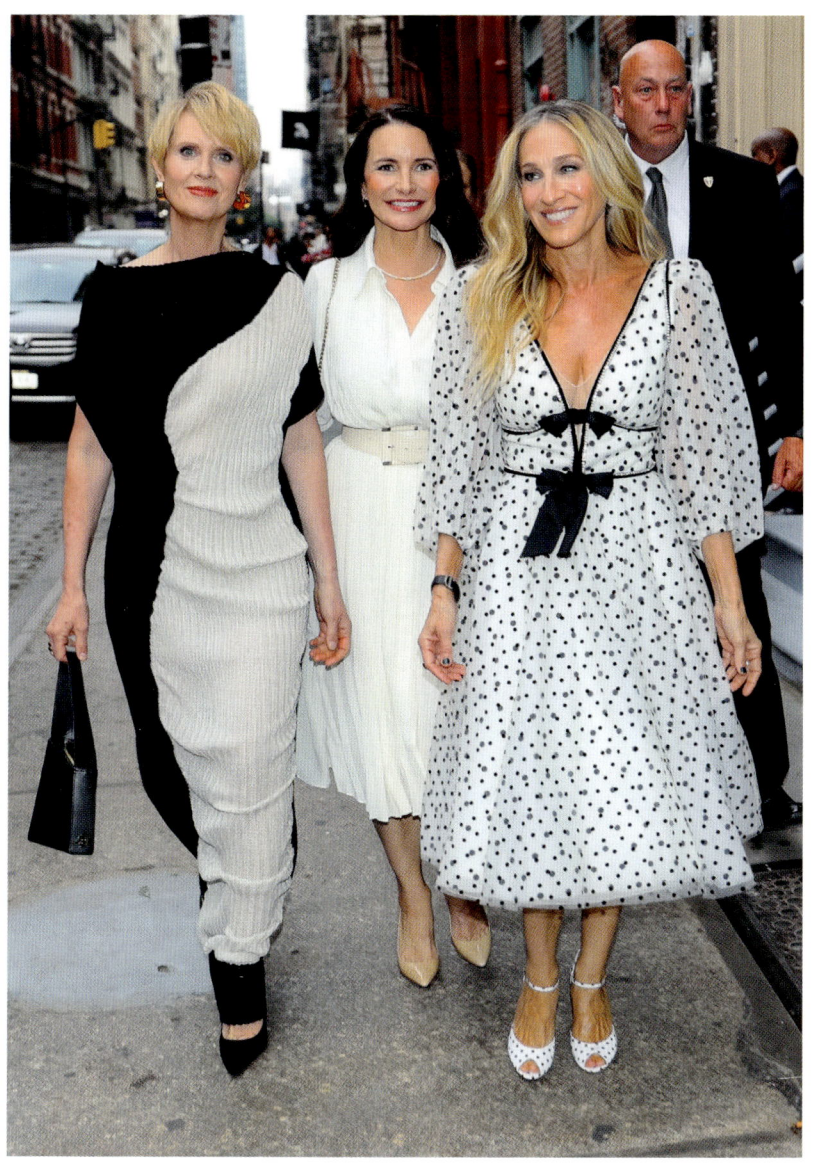

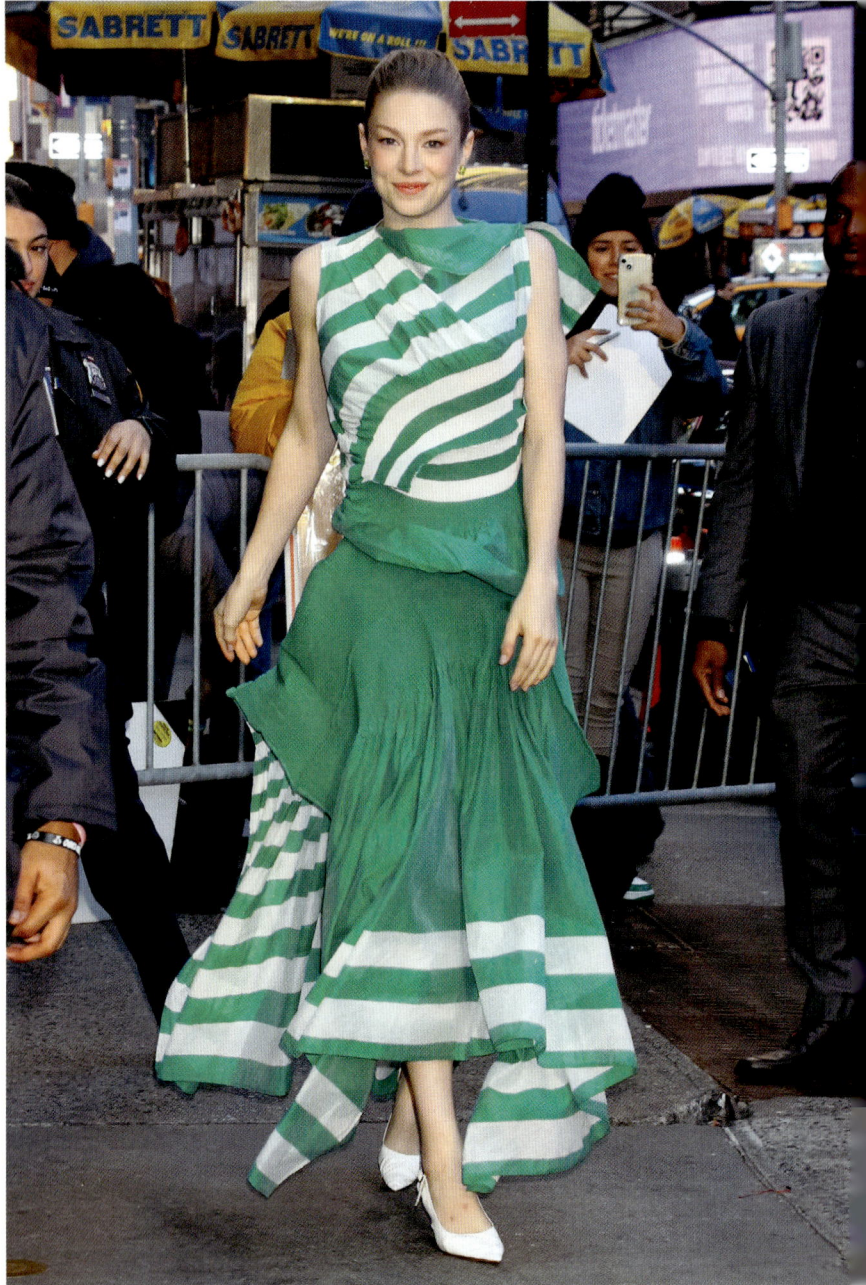

identifiable on the front row for her trademark quiff as much for her penchant for wearing Pleats Please, usually in purple. The brand has also been adopted by a new generation of style-conscious stars, including basketball player Russell Westbrook and two-time Oscar-winning actor Mahershala Ali.

More recently, a printed jumpsuit by Miyake made an appearance on *And Just Like That…,* HBO Max's sequel to *Sex and the City*, where it was worn by the Upper East Side mom played by Nicole Ari Parker. Actor Cynthia Nixon wore a dress from Issey Miyake's Spring/Summer 2023 collection when she attended a private celebration for the 25th anniversary of *Sex and the City* in New York in June 2023. Actor and model Hunter Schafer made headlines when she wore a dress from Issey Miyake's Autumn/Winter 2023 collection on US TV show *Good Morning America* in November 2023.

In an unexpected turn, celebrities also favour wearing Miyake at glitzy events. Entrepreneur and former actor Mary-Kate Olsen wore Issey Miyake to the annual CFDA Fashion Awards in 2013. At the 2022 Grammy Awards, both Joni Mitchell and Anthony Roth Costanzo wore pleated looks. Italian singer Malika Ayane wore Issey Miyake to the 80th Venice International Film Festival in 2023. Actor and singer Cynthia Erivo wore Issey Miyake to the 49th Chaplin Award Gala honouring Jeff Bridges in April 2024.

The brand continues to be met with adoration in magazines: Japanese drag queen and TV personality Mitz Mangrove shared their love for Bao Bao bags in a quirky interview and shoot for *Vogue Japan* in June 2023. The publication also featured actor, filmmaker and humanitarian Angelina Jolie wearing Issey Miyake on the cover of its July 2024 issue.

Despite Miyake's astonishing body of work, it was a quiet end for the designer (a public service following his passing

OPPOSITE Hunter Schafer wearing a dress from A/W 2023 for her appearance on *Good Morning America.*

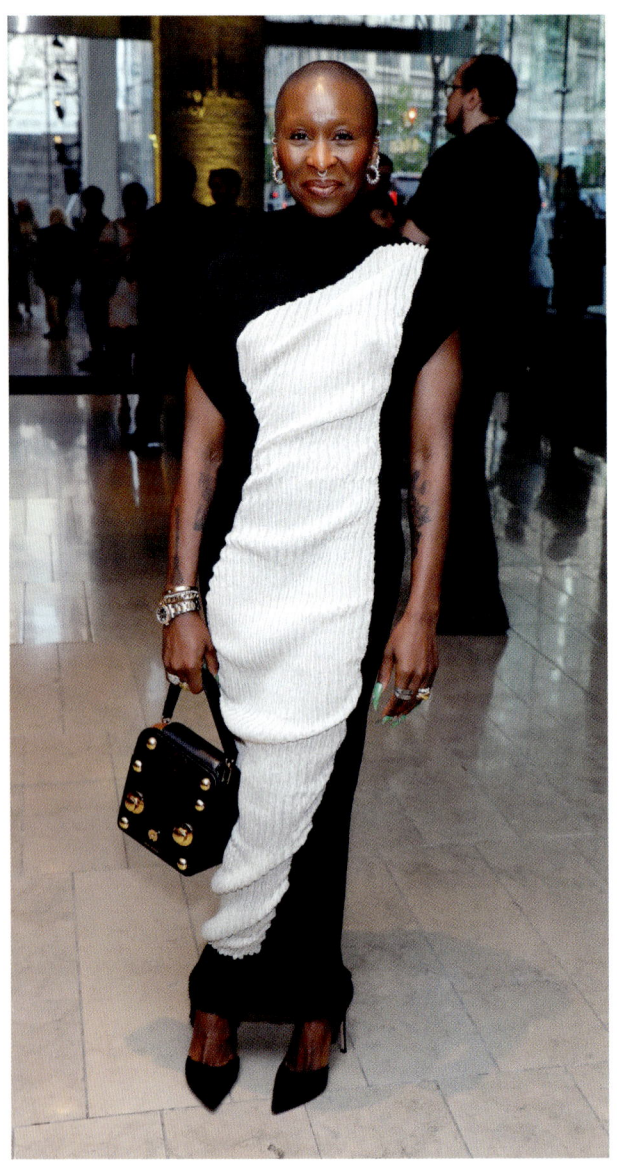

LEFT Cynthia
Erivo wears Issey
Miyake to the 49th
Chaplin Award
Gala honouring
Jeff Bridges in New
York, 2024.

OPPOSITE Mary-
Kate Olsen arrives
at the 2013 CFDA
Fashion Awards in
New York wearing
Issey Miyake.

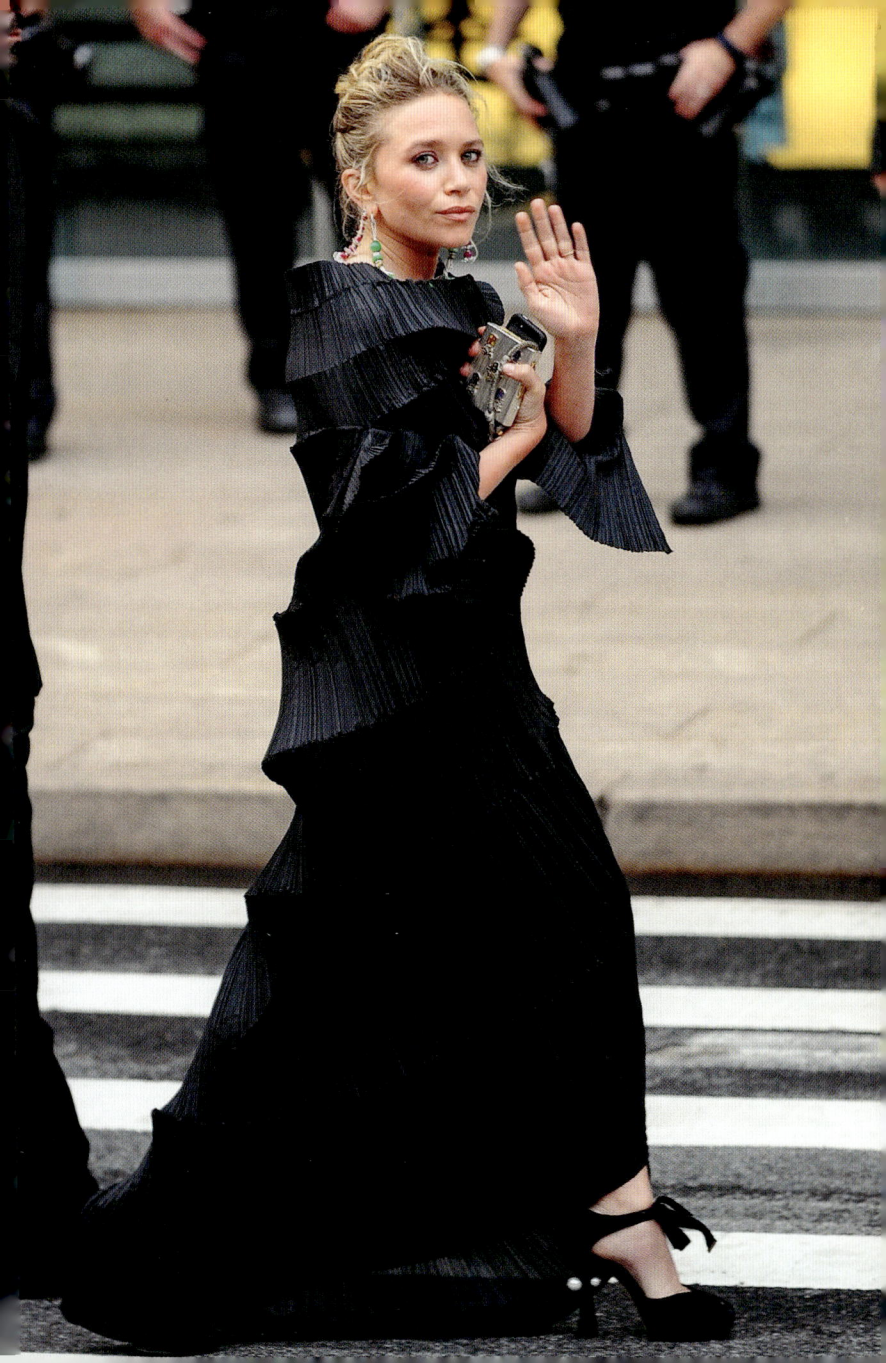

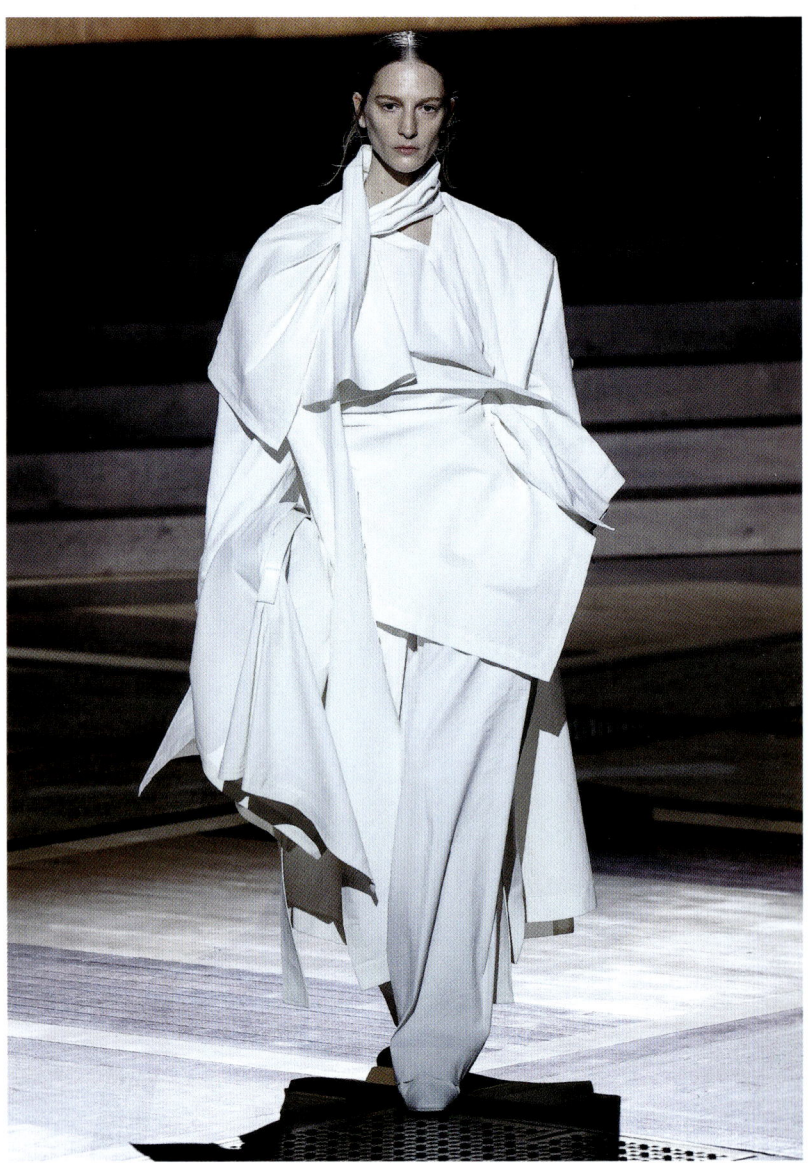

OPPOSITE
Womenswear A/W
2024.

BELOW Satoshi
Kondo at the show
for S/S 2025.

was not held, in accordance with his wishes). Nonetheless, his iconoclastic values and the brilliance of his technological precision continue to have a lasting impact across multiple industries. After all, Miyake was more than a fashion designer – he was an architect, an engineer and a humanitarian, whose deeply creative body of work transcended proportion and form, as well as gender, size and age.

Asked in 1999 whether he aspired for his designs to be timeless, Miyake responded: "I don't think about that when I make my clothes. The designers who will be remembered in the next century will be those who have created some kind of fundamental form, like Chanel, Poiret or Vionnet." Miyake, arguably, achieved more than that with his body of work, offering lasting proof of what borderless thinking and experimentation can achieve.

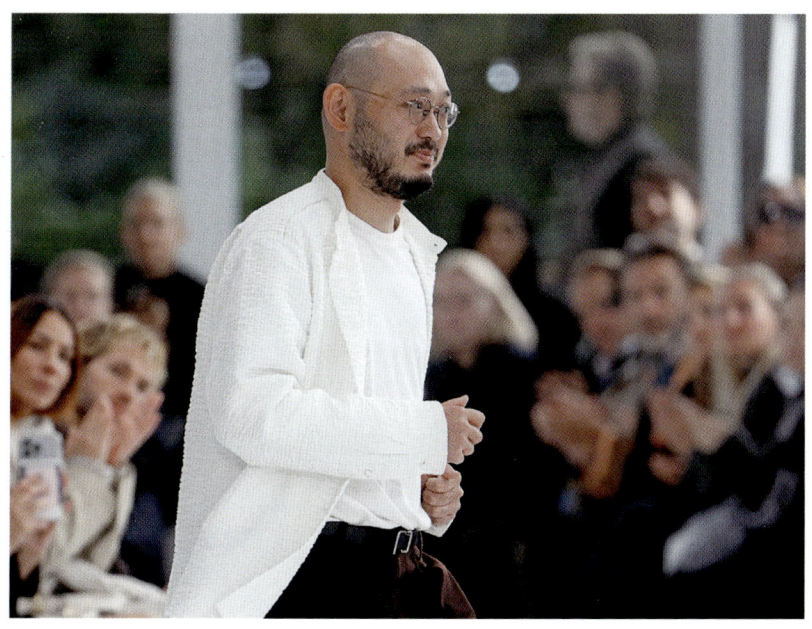

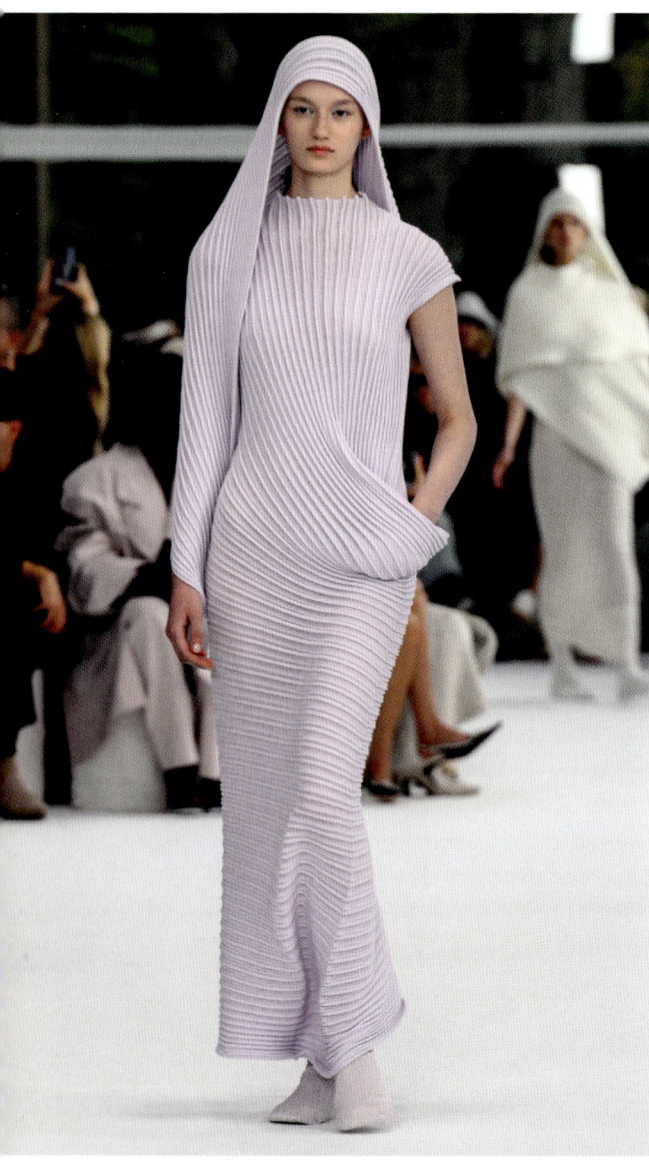

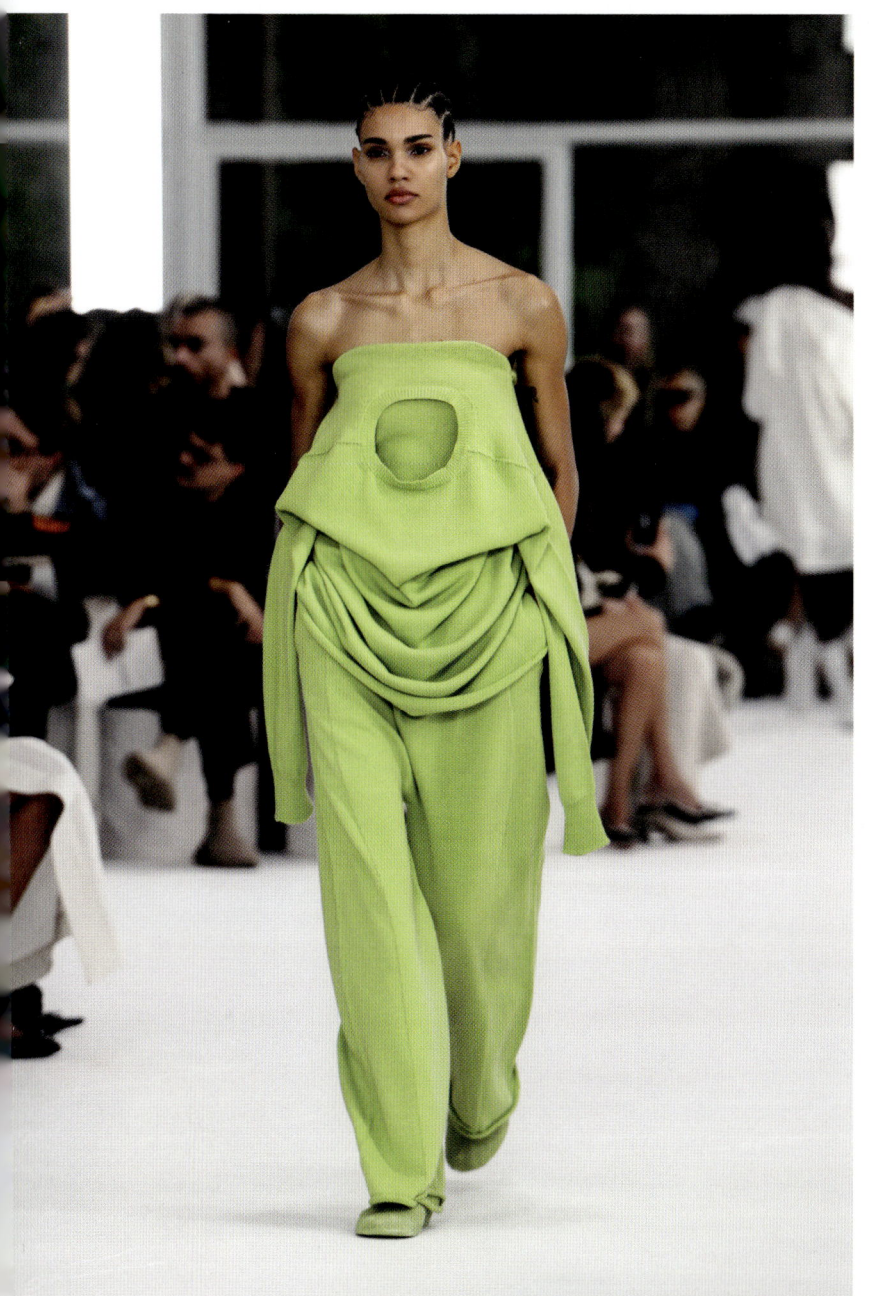

INDEX

CREDITS

The publishers would like to thank the following sources for their kind permission to reproduce the pictures in this book.